Graphic Design New York 2

Gra
Des
N
Gra
Des
N
York

Graphic Design: New York 2

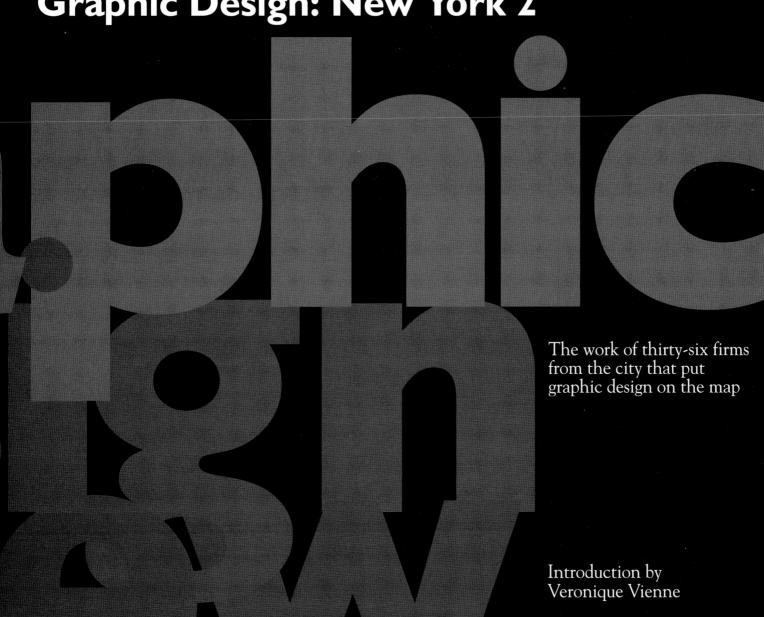

The work of thirty-six firms
from the city that put
graphic design on the map

Introduction by
Veronique Vienne

Organized by
Michael Bierut,
William Drenttel
and DK Holland

Produced by
The Pushpin Group

Published by
Rockport/Allworth Editions
Rockport Publishers, Inc.
Allworth Press

Distributed by
North Light Books
Cincinnati, Ohio

First published in the United States by Rockport/Allworth
Editions, a trade name of Rockport Publishers, Inc. and
Allworth Press.

Rockport Publishers, Inc.
146 Granite Street
Rockport, Massachusetts 01966
Telephone: 508 546 9590
Facsimile: 508 546 7141

Allworth Press
10 East 23rd Street
New York, NY 10010
Telephone: 212 777 8395
Facsimile: 212 777 8261

Distribution to the book and art trade in the United States
and Canada by: North Light Books, an imprint of:

F&W Publications
1507 Dana Avenue
Cincinnati, Ohio 45207
Telephone: 1 800 289 0963

Distributed to the book and art trade throughout the rest
of the world by: Rockport Publishers, Inc.
Rockport, Massachusetts 01966

ISBN: 1-56496-297-0
Printed in China

Table of Contents

Acknowledgements *vi*
Dedication *vii*
About This Book by DK Holland *ix*

Refusing the Hype by Veronique Vienne *x*

Alexander Isley Design *1*
Bates Hori *7*
Bernhardt Fudyma *13*
Blue Brick *19*
Calori & Vanden-Eynden, Ltd. *25*
Carin Goldberg *31*
Carla Hall Design Group, Inc. *37*

Looking for movement in shadow;
the power of an empty chamber. Mews Muse.
A visual essay by Bates Hori *43*

Chermayeff & Geismar Inc. *45*
Desgrippes Gobé & Associates *51*
Design/Writing/Research *57*
Diana DeLucia Design, Ltd. *63*
Donovan and Green *69*
Drenttel Doyle Partners *75*
Eric Baker Design Associates *81*

No. Radio
A visual essay by Carin Golberg *87*

Frankfurt Balkind Partners *89*
Jessica Helfand Studios *95*
Landor Associates *101*
Louise Fili Ltd. *107*
Michael Ian Kaye *113*
Mirko Ilić *119*
Number Seventeen *125*

A Buggy Ride Through NYC.
A visual essay by James Victore *131*

Parham Santana Design *133*
Paul Davis Studio *139*
Pentagram *145*
Pushpin *151*
Sagmeister Inc. *157*
Siegel & Gale *163*
Slatoff + Cohen Partners *169*
Slover [AND] Company *175*

Coming Back from the Printer
A visual essay by Paul Davis *181*

Smart Design *183*
Studio Morris *189*
Two Twelve Associates, Inc. *195*
Victore Design Works *201*
Vignelli Associates *207*
Waters Design Associates, Inc. *213*
Wood Design *219*

Acknowledgements

It was Tad Crawford of Allworth Press who conceived the idea of a series of books about the work of graphic designers. The first book, published in 1992, is titled *Graphic Design: New York—The Work of 39 Great Graphic Design Firms from the City That Put Graphic Design on the Map.*

GDNY's success created such a high visibility for graphic design that it led us to conceive *Graphic Design: America—The Work of Twenty-eight Design Firms from Across the United States and Canada* (volume two is also coming out this year). Others are: *Signs and Spaces—A Survey of the Environmental Graphic Design Work of Twenty-two Major International Design Firms* and *Design in Depth—Unique Projects Created, Visually Explored and Analyzed by Fifty-one Leading Design Firms.* Of course the next natural step was the need to educate the world about illustration, so we created *Illustration: America—Outstanding Portfolios,* which was published in 1996.

Tad had the vision to include Rockport Publishers as co-publishers of the book. Rockport Publishers' Stan Patey and Arthur Furst lent their invaluable publishing and sales expertise and wisdom throughout the project.

Thank you to Scott Gilbertson who assisted with the book's initial design processes, and Matt Verssue: both helped to contact the design firms in the beginning when they were students at the University of Kansas. Janet Shaeffer and Patty Swinney, also of KU, devoted many hours working on the organizational aspects of the book.

A special thank you to Julie Hillemeyer and Rebecca Horowitz. Julie and Rebecca started on the book while students of the University of Kansas and continued on at Pushpin to complete the project after graduation. Julie was the primary designer of the entire book. She reworked the grid and style from the first volume in hopes to both update and better display all the firms' work. During the final process, Julie brought the book back to her hometown of St. Louis and, working under a tight deadline, finished the color-proofing process with a dedication that is unmatched. Rebecca Horowitz copy edited this book, creating the style and controlling its content. Both coordinated and kept track of all the firms throughout the design of the book, as well as completed its production: Julie and Rebecca put in countless hours, nights and weekends in a tireless team effort geared towards achieving the best book possible.

Dedication

an Friedman was a graphic designer, intellectual and enigma: Dan designed the Citicorp logo while at Anspach Grossman Portugal, and was the first designer at Pentagram in New York to work under Colin Forbes. He, with his then-wife—designer April Grieman—are credited with the invention of the New Wave design movement in one of the most defining eras of graphic design. This book is dedicated to the memory of a vital man stricken by AIDS; one who managed to create a lot of waves during his brief stay on this earth.

About This Book

I n 1990, Michael Beirut, William Drenttel and I set out to create the first major anthology of contemporary New York City designers' works. The invitation to graphic designers to join us was a rallying cry: The city had long been the center for design in the United States, and displaying the array of richness in the work of 39 of the top firms was our way of declaring that New York was still in a leadership role.

Graphic Design: New York was published in 1992 and was immediately a commercial success: worldwide sales demonstrated the depth of interest in New York design. Importantly, the book also became useful reference for clients, libraries and students alike.

New York, the clichéd, fast-paced city: it became evident that a second volume of *Graphic Design: New York* would serve not only as a show-case for new work, but work from new firms, confirming the field's rapid expansion in ground breaking and varied media.

Moreover, the publication of *Graphic Design: America* by Rockport Publishers in 1994 had showed that many parts of the United States could brag about design talent. And so it seemed fitting to revisit the New York scene to see what changes had occurred in the intervening years. This book, *Graphic Design: New York 2*, is the result.

Although we started with a clean slate, in selecting the 36 firms for this volume, many of the firms from the first volume continued to be on the top of our list. But, firms had emerged in the few years between volumes, as had new individuals.

Other changes are of note: firms that had focused on editorial design are now doing innovative corporate design because the corporate mindset had changed about design, both new and established design firms were struggling to find their niche in this new media.

The evolution of the marketplace for graphic design as a field is clearly creating new challenges for design as a creative endeavor, as well as sprouting issues relating to professional practices and design/client relationships.

The selection of designers in *Graphic Design: New York 2* expresses the range of talent working in New York today: big firm or boutique; idiosyncratic or concept and marketing-driven in content.

New York is still the biggest and most challenging market for graphic design in the United States, perhaps the world, today.

DK Holland

Refusing the Hype

Graphic Design: New York 2. Don't let the deceptively plain title of this book mislead you: this compendium of portfolios isn't a mere industry who's who. It is a lot more than that. When they agreed to be included in this retrospective, the daring Gothamites featured here chose to make a definite statement. By electing to describe their work simply as "graphic design," they decided to take a stand and transcend the emerging hype.

Graphic design used to be an invisible activity, part of the services offered by printers. We've come a long way since the days when layouts were done by anonymous artists usually known as typesetters. Whereas it took years of training for these silent craftsmen to learn to compose a page, it now takes about two hours—if that much—for young, media-savvy techno-cubs to learn the rudiments of computer graphics. Before the ink is dry on their business card, this new e-generation can—and does—produce graphic work of surprising allure and far-reaching cultural significance.

While the craft of graphic design is becoming more accessible—and thus more popular—its practice, in contrast, is gaining in complexity. Today, successful graphic designers do more than simply engage readers with their deft handling of printed words and images; they also think like—and for—their clients, targeting their visual messages to specific audiences; they keep up with the latest multimedia developments to assess new marketing opportunities; last but not least, they try to figure out ways of helping the entire print-based industry negotiate the transition into the interactive information age.

Attempts are being made to redefine the role of graphic design in our culture by changing its name. Heirs to Gutenberg, people who practice his art know better than underestimate the visual impact of printed words. Yet, these communication mavericks become linguistically challenged when describing on paper what it is they do for a living. Cryptic blurbs printed on self-promotion brochures and designers' collateral material attest to the scope of this identity crisis.

What, for example, is the difference between a firm that offers marketing strategy & image management and a competitor who specializes in brand equity development? And how does that compare with visual communication and identity design systems? Eager to project a megabyte image, yet another category of graphic digitari call themselves information architects, emerging media artists or graphic content providers.

In this Babel-like context, describing what you do as "graphic design" amounts to an act of sang-froid. The thirty-six firms in this book showed great poise and self-restraint when they decided to drop the epistemological act and rally under the old tried-and-true name. In doing so, they renewed with a literate tradition that used to be one of the main accouterment of the profession. From the Egyptian scribe with his stylus and papyrus to the contemporary editor clicking away on an ergonomically-correct keyboard, people who manipulate text have always had an irreducible love for words.

In fact, some of the youngest firms in New York, like Drenttel Doyle Partners, Design/Writing/Research, Bates Hori, Alexander Isley Design and Slatoff+Cohen Partners are making no apologies today for their intellectual approach to design. For them, finding the right words to define a project is equivalent to coming up with the right idea. Like all the participants in this book, they would rather debate the accuracy of a particular visual language than the relevance of an image. In this atmosphere of new objectivism, nothing could be more satisfying than the "graphic design" label. Let it be known that the word graphic means specific, lucid and unequivocal.

SO, WHILE OTHER CREATIVE TYPES

in this town, from architects to makeup artists, would do anything to get media attention, graphic designers deliberately shun the limelight. It's not a case of modesty, mind you. Their publicity-shy behavior is the expression of a more evolved form of hubris. They think of themselves as artists—not merchants.

There is a historical precedent for what some people think is a delusion of grandeur. The best-known graphic designers in New York have always been artists—either painters, collagists, sculptors or conceptual artists. Among them are Peter Max, Milton Glaser, Seymour Chwast, Paul Davis, Ivan Chermayeff, Keith Haring and,

more recently, Dan Friedman, Tibor and Maira Kalman, and James Victore. It makes sense. In this town, street art, displayed either on walls, buses or newsstands, gets top billing. Graphic artists who produce graffiti, illustrate posters and get their work on magazine covers attract more attention than their peers who operate within the business community.

Just as influential—but not household names by any means—are corporate-savvy graphic designers who manage to be ubiquitous in other ways. Sometimes, even their work is in your face. For starters, there is Frankfurt Balkind Partners' ESPN logo; Landor Associates' FedEx brand repositioning; Donovan & Green's corporate identity for Sony; Parham Santana Design's packaging for CBS/Fox Video; Slover & Co.'s advertising for Saks Fifth Avenue; Two Twelve Associates' work for the Citibank ATM system; Siegel and Gale's Metro Card program; Desgrippes Gobé Associates' Fila campaign; Number Seventeen's controversial advertisement for VH-1. And the list goes on, and on, and on. Graphic designers need not promote who they are and what they do—for them, good design is the best revenge.

An odd fixation, the pursuit of good design, is the one thing that characterizes New York graphic designers. Other design professionals will tell you that, in this competitive environment, good isn't good enough. Fashion designers, for example, don't want their work to be perceived as good—they want it to be "hot." Advertising art directors dread the idea of being merely good—their survival depends on being "cool." As for decorators, they would be mortified if they were described as good—these people want to be "utterly elegant."

But as far as graphic designers are concerned, "good design" says it all. The expression was coined by the Museum of Modern Art after World War II, with a series of "Good Design" shows displaying the best examples of contemporary Modernist graphic and industrial design. Soon the expression good design became, in the international language, synonymous with museum-quality graphic work.

During the prosperous 1950s and 1960s, corporate America embraced the MOMA concept, declaring that "Good Design is Good Business." The endorsement was somewhat self-serving: In the postwar era, most companies were reconverting their manufacturing from armament to consumer goods and needed a complete image makeover. Good design—as approved by the Art establishment—gave them instant credibility and cachet.

International-Style, Swiss-inspired, corporate identity systems helped American corporations establish themselves here and abroad. Some of the most elegant and vigorous innovative graphic work was done in New York at the time: while William Golden and Lou Dorfsman were reshaping the corporate culture of CBS, Paul Rand was packaging IBM, and Chermayeff and Geismar were designing new identity systems for Mobil and Chase Manhattan.

But the 1970s and 1980s challenged the belief that good design and commerce were compatible bedfellows. It happened sometime between the lunar landing and the Watergate break-in: we lost our faith in the timeless perfection of pure form and function. Although good design was still officially sanctioned, it was no longer critical to the growth of the economy. In fact, good design was beginning to be perceived as too static, too sedate and much too enduring. In the post-Vietnam war era, more consumer spending was needed and new incentives had to be invented. Little by little, the concept of "style" emerged as the solution. Yes style—the champion of built-in obsolescence and the arch-enemy of good design.

For a generation of graphic designers who still revered the likes of Alvin Lustig and Bradbury Thompson, these were trying times. Avant Garde had replaced Helvetica and decorative fonts were the rage. Sneaking good design past clients soon became quite a challenge.

The most aggressive designers took action: they shaved their beard, retired their tweed jackets and put away their jeans. They exchanged their artiste garb for trendy haircuts, expensive Italian suits and European designer glasses. In conference rooms that now looked like screening rooms, they served cappuccinos to clients. And if by chance, their corporate sponsors chose to implement a "good design" solution, the Armani-clad graphic designer was now very careful not to betray his pleasure with a show of emotion.

Explicit concern for good design was banished from the practice. Emulating advertising agencies, large design firms hired marketing executives and created project management teams to handle client contact. In some extreme cases, people with no design background were put in charge of the business. In the meantime, senior designers, who were nostalgic for the days of Will Burtin and Alex Brodovitch, were kept in the studio; young graphic designers, who couldn't spell Seymour Chwast, were taken to meetings, exposed to clients and groomed to speak the language of nouveau design marketing.

Suddenly everyone in the office was a communication expert. Problem-solving, not typographical excellence, was the main topic of conversation between designers. There was a lot of talk about graphic solutions, conceptual platforms and visual strategies. Old timers had to mind their p's and q's. Some brash designers even went as far as proclaiming in public their misgivings about "good design for the sake of good design."

What fools these mortals be. New York graphic designers resisted the trend as long as they could. In the early 1980s, at long last, some newly established studios began to produce work that looked appropriately "stylish." Nothing as exuberant as the retro and vernacular stuff done in Memphis, San Francisco or Minneapolis, but it was a pretty good try for the Big Apple. With a highly personal design approach camouflaged under fashionable Post-Modern rhetoric,

Paula Scher, Louise Fili, Carin Goldberg and Lorraine Louie helped create a sense of chic excitement. Yet, the truth be told, their work was too good to be faddish. It never quite captured the allure of obsolescence.

Contrary to popular belief, it takes a lot of maturity to stay on the cutting edge of a profession. While graphic designers in other parts of the country are still dealing with issues of adolescence by creating work that's as pesky as it is arresting, in New York newness doesn't make news. Greater levels of sophistication are expected of everyone. From Landor with its 350 employees to James Victore who prefers to work from his apartment, all graphic designers compete for the same Fortune 500 clients. Here, the common denominator is obviously not form—it's content.

THIS BOOK IS A TESTIMONY
to the failure of New York graphic designers to truly embrace the concept of style. Don't peruse its pages in search of the definitive hip New York "look." You won't find it. Sorry. All you are likely to stumble on is good design.

Veronique Vienne
Brooklyn, New York
June 1996

Alexander Isley Design

Principal: Alexander Isley
Year Founded: 1988
Size of Firm: 9
Key Clients: American Museum of the Moving Image, Canon USA, Champion International, Forbes, Inc.; Giorgio Armani, MTV Networks, Nickelodeon, Reebok International, The Rock and Roll Hall of Fame and Museum, Sony Wonder, Time Warner, The Voyager Company.

580 Broadway
Suite 715
New York, NY 10012
212 941 7945

Alexander Isley founded his firm to, as he says, "Give me the chance to work on as many different things as possible." His strategy has paid off, as he and his staff of designers have been commissioned to design everything from shoe boxes to museum exhibitions. Recently, the firm completed the design of an architectural graphics program for The Rock and Roll Hall of Fame, and the creation of interiors and merchandising materials for the WH Smith chain of retail stores. Even though the scope of the studio's work is varied, the thoughtfulness and wit that the designers bring to each assignment is constant. "One could argue that we spend way too much time at the beginning of an assignment talking to our clients and asking lots of pesky questions, but I think that's the most important part of the design process," says Isley. "The biggest mistake a designer can make is rushing to a visual solution. We should decide what something should look like only after deciding what it should *do*."

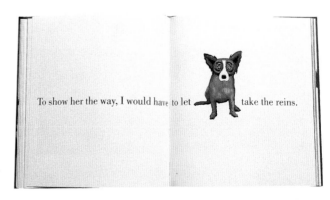

Cover and book design of *Blue Dog*, a book featuring the "Blue Dog" paintings of George Rodrigue, for Viking Studio Books, New York, NY. Filled with surprises, inside the book are pages with disappearing type, a dog hologram, and an effect where a black and white dog turns blue. The slipcase cover is designed so that the dog's eyes peek out. The first edition sold out in 10 days.
Art Director, Alexander Isley; designer, Lynette Cortez; writer, Lawrence S. Freundlich.

right
Left to right: Veronica Burke, Lisa Billard, David Albertson, Alexander Isley (seated), Julia Wargaski, Penny Blatt, Gabrielle Dubois-Pellerin and Eva Keller.
Photography, Ray Charles White

right
"Shoukichi Kina" poster for Luaka Bop Records/ Central Park Summer Stage, New York, NY. The poster promotes the performance of an Okinawan funk band in Central Park.
Art Director, Alexander Isley; designer, David Albertson.

right
Display for Nickelodeon/ Sony Wonder, New York, NY. The point-of-purchase display for video retailers is a stand featuring three-dimensional characters designed to fold down into an easy to assemble self-shipper.
Art Director, Alexander Isley; designer, Jamie Reeves.

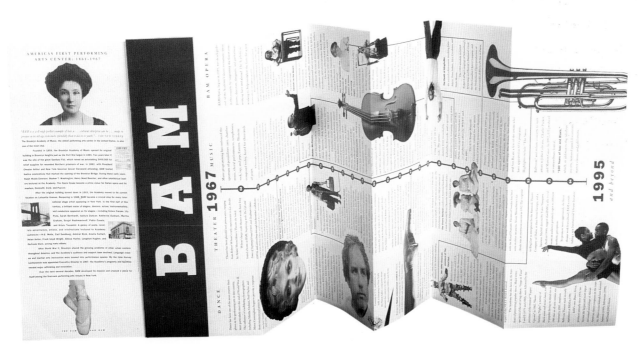

left
Fundraising brochure for Brooklyn Academy of Music, Brooklyn, NY. In order to provide a visual focus to the piece, an accordion-fold time-line was created, highlighting a history of the Academy's programming. The BAM logo on the front cover is based on the mosaic lettering on the floor of the main theater's lobby.
Art Director, Alexander Isley; designer, Melinda Beck; editor, Willem Brans, C.W. Shaver & Co.

left

Brochure for Canon USA, Lake Success, New York. Created in association with Dentsu America. The design is a pair of 32-page brochures featuring highlights and product listings for the corporation's year in review. The design was created to provide a spirited interpretation of technical corporate sales and marketing information. Using the word "able" helped to reaffirm Canon's position as a leader in the design of consumer and business equipment. Art Director, Alexander Isley; designer, David Albertson; writer, Mike Campanella; photography, Hugh Kretchmer.

Graphic identity for Bolo Restaurant, New York, NY. Design of the logo, menu, exterior signage and interior wall murals for a restaurant featuring Spanish-influenced food. The graphic look was reflective of the food— bright, vibrant, and with a Spanish twist. The murals were created from hand-cut, custom silk-screened sheets of 4-by-6 foot paper, arranged to be reminiscent of brightly-colored street posters.

Art Director, Alexander Isley; designers, Philip Bratter and Jamie Reeves; architect, James Biber, Pentagram.

"Packaging the New" exhibition graphics for Cooper-Hewitt National Design Museum, New York, NY. A visual identity program for an exhibition examining the roles of marketers, advertisers and industrial designers in the development and selling of consumer products. It included the design of both interior and exterior exhibition graphics. Art Director, Alexander Isley; designer, Melinda Beck; exhibit designer, Constantin Boym; curator, Gail Davidson.

left
Exterior site signage for the exhibition.

bottom left
Stack of custom designed cereal boxes indicating the entrance to the exhibit.

bottom right
An interior time-line for the exhibition, tracking the development of product advertising and the exhibition brochure.

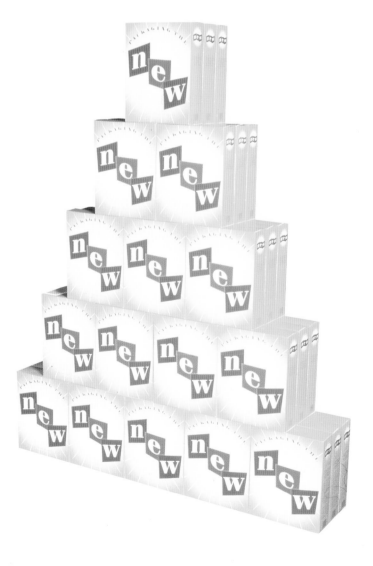

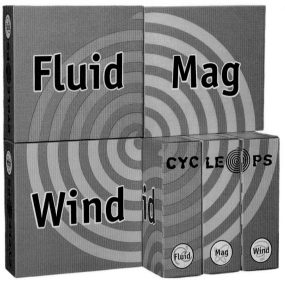

Designing Your Future

Compare the Series 500 phone with the phones you use. What features are the same? What features are different? Why have phone designs changed? How would you evaluate the phones you use today? How would you improve them?

What might telephones do for you in the future? Design one.

Who will use your telephone and where? How will it work and look? Will it have special features? What will be the power source and materials? What will you call it?

Whatever you design, you will start back at the beginning of the process: defining the PROBLEM.

Design **finishes** with a SOLUTION

5 MAKING
The designers proposed a new kind of plastic for the final product because it could be molded, making manufacturing efficient and cost-effective. Also, this plastic was lightweight but durable and came in many colors. AT&T agreed and mass-produced 25 million phones from this one design! They called it the "Series 500."

4 EVALUATING
Based on the models, the designer and client could see how the phone would fit the user's hand and ear. They then created prototypes to test the performance of the whole phone. Together, they determined the final design.

3 SHOWING
The designers created models of wood and clay to give form to their ideas for the phone's handset, base, and dial. They also used models and drawings to share their ideas with the client, AT&T.

2 SKETCHING
The designer used sketches, like quick notes, to envision, develop and evaluate new ideas.

1 THINKING
The design team began by defining the problem. They studied how phones were made, how they looked, and how people used them. They identified many problems that could be solved through a new design.

Then, the team challenged their imaginations through a brainstorming exercise. They played with all possibilities for a new phone design: What if we changed the shape? What if all the edges were rounded? What if we added color?

HENRY DREYFUSS
Industrial Designer

In 1946, Bell Telephone Labs (AT&T) asked designer Henry Dreyfuss to improve the phone used in millions of American homes and offices. The designer and his team used the following process to respond to this challenge.

WHAT NEEDED TO BE IMPROVED?
These were the problems that needed to be fixed on the phones that people were using before 1946.

Design **starts** with a PROBLEM

WHAT IS DESIGN?

Design is the process we use to shape the world and everything in it: products, packaging, clothing, buildings, landscapes, communications, transportation, and cities. Design responds to people's changing needs, to new technologies, and to the environment.

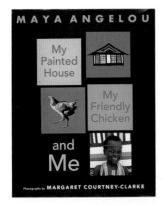

left and below left
Design of Maya Angelou's, *My Painted House, My Friendly Chicken and Me* for Clarkson N. Potter, New York, NY. The children's book, incorporating photographs of South Africa's Ndebele tribe, is free-form and exuberant—created to reflect the rhythm and cadence of the narrative. Designer, Alexander Isley; photography, Margaret Courtney-Clarke.

left and below
Architectural signage program for The Rock and Roll Hall of Fame and Museum, Cleveland, OH. The program was designed to reflect the building's architectural style, and was created in association with Calori & Vanden-Eynden, Ltd., New York, NY. Designers, Alexander Isley, David Albertson, Chris Calori and David Vanden-Eynden.

above
Private label magnets. The refrigerator magnets, packaged as a set, are grouped by theme to increase desirability as gift items. The sets shown are representative samples from over 50 magnet sets that the studio has created to date. The magnets are sold in stores across the US, Europe and Japan. Art Director, Alexander Isley; designers, Gabrielle Dubois-Pelerin, Eva Keller and Lourdes Bañez; manufactured by Blue Q, Pittsfield, MA.

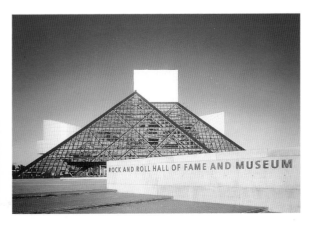

Bates Hori

Principals: Richard Bates,
Allen Hori
Year Founded: 1993
Size of Firm: 2
Key Clients: Absolut
Vodka, Atlantic Records,
David Leinheardt
Management, ID Magazine,
Prescriptives, Westcott
Fenasci Design Group.

251 West 19th Street
1E
New York, NY 10011
212 691 6381

ates Hori is a studio dedicated to the poetics of design and the resiliency of intellect. The two designers (plus studio muses Book and Myth) are interested in the exploration of developing technologies and the possibilities in joining image and sound. The desire to communicate a richer, more humanized message surfaces through their graphics. "So often in reading a text or a piece of art, what is not explicitly there may be more telling than what is there. For media designers Richard Bates and Allen Hori, this shadowland—the interstice that exists between their talents and personalities—is the nexus of their newly formed studio, Bates Hori," *I.D. Magazine* ("Top Forty" Jan/Feb 1995). Published and exhibited internationally, the firm has won numerous awards for its ability to provide factual and atmospheric meaning to its graphic communication.

above
Christmas card for Lifebeat, the music industry's organization to fight AIDS, New York, NY. The card shows fantasy, love, hope—even in a time when AIDS is a primary concern—love is still as pure as a fairy tale. Designer, Richard Bates; photography, Bates and Melanie Nissen.

left
Richard Bates and
Allen Hori.
Headshot photography,
Melanie Nissen; portrait
photography,
Ray Charles White.

above left
Poster for Lifebeat. The image communicates the need for a change in attitudes, as well as solicit money to effect change. Designer, Richard Bates; photography, Allen Hori.

left
Book for the fiber department at the Cranbrook Academy of Art, Bloomfield Hills, MI. The book features the work and biographies of 18 students in fibers. Designer/photography; Richard Bates.

above
CD cover design for Atlantic Records, New York, NY. The music derives from heartfelt storytelling, dealing with isolation, loss and human reflection. The cover, "Get Me Out of Here," portrays the vignetted state of mind, and the typography attempts to provide a pointer/directional sign in the roadside landscape. Designer, Allen Hori. photography, Micheal McLaughlin.

Paper promo, designer series for Potlatch Corp., Cloquet, MN. The project addressed music and sound in a poetic, mythical way. It also weaved this designer's "take" on the music industry, promoted the paper's recycled content, and contributed to the reduction of paper waste. The piece produced no waste in terms of trimming—the press sheet was the piece in its entirety. Designers, Allen Hori, Charlie Becker and Rob Eberhardt; language, Augustine Hope; photography, Hori and Gaye Chan.

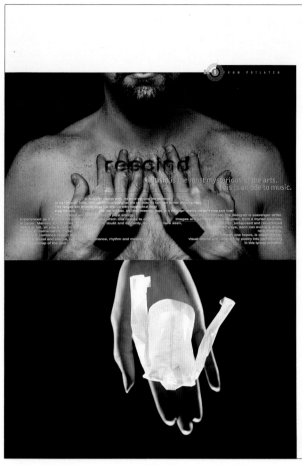

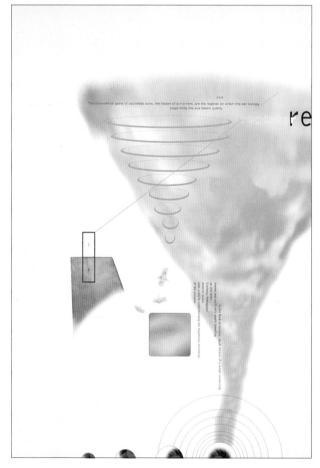

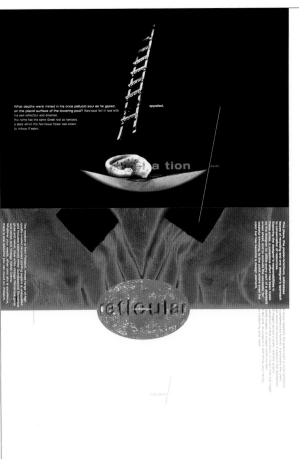

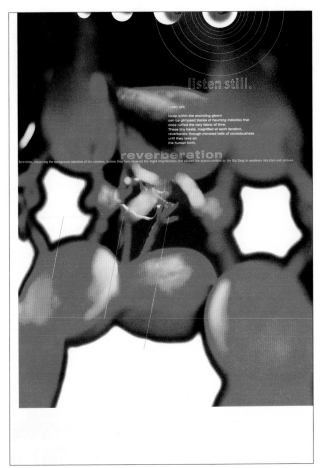

top right
Invitation/announcement
for Westcott Fenasci Design
Group, New York, NY. The
project introduced the
launch of a fashion design
company. The idea was
pushed to utilize high construction and severe aes-
thetics in its premier line.
Pedestrian symbols of
"construction" and "warn-
ing" were used throughout
the series.
Designer, Allen Hori;
photography, Bill Orcutt.

top far right
Ad for ID Magazine, New
York, NY. The Absolut
Vodka ad references ideas
specific to a design audience.
Designer, Richard Bates;
photography, Allen Hori
and Bill Orcutt.

bottom right
Announcement of an art
exhibit at the Detroit Artist
Market, Detroit, MI. The
invitations were printed on
top of the previous exhibit
invitations, drawing issues
of the current show into
the announcement itself.
Designer/photography,
Richard Bates.

bottom far right
Output 2, a continuing series
of publications targeted for
designers, Cranbrook
Academy of Art, Bloomfield
Hills, MI. The publication
is an ideology of experimentation and investigation of
both form and content. It
proved to be a successful
tool in sparking discussion
and reaction to the central
idea of randomness and
information bombardment.
Designers, Richard Bates,
Michael Hall, David
Shields, Brian Smith and
Susanna Stieff.

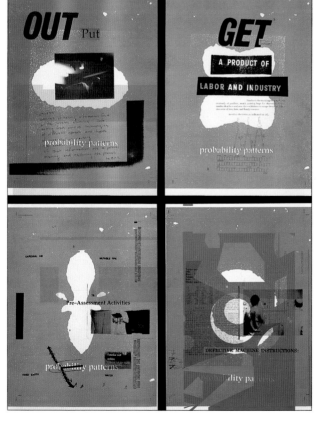

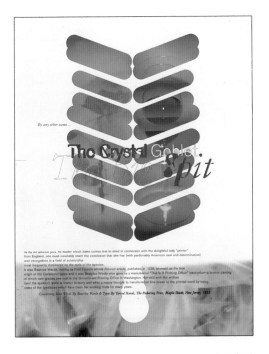

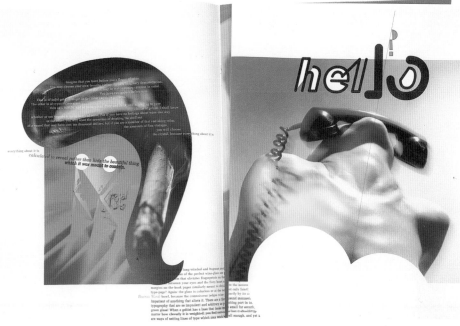

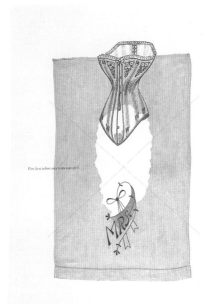

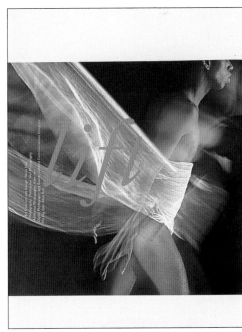

above
Paper promo in *Rethinking Design II*, for Mohawk Paper, New York, NY. It is a designer's response and interpretation of a concept, The Crystal Goblet. It provided a pointed opinion through text and image. The project addressed issues of clarity and obscurity via a visual discussion of gender identity and stereotypical positioning of culturally empowered roles, which parallel the text's critique of designers and typography. Designer, Allen Hori; photography, Hori and Chris Weil.

Bernhardt Fudyma Design Group, Inc.

Principals: Craig Bernhardt, Janice Fudyma
Year Founded: 1973
Size of Firm: 8
Key Clients: American International Group (AIG), Bankers Trust, Bear Stearns, Citibank, Gilbert Paper Company, IBM, John Wiley & Sons, MasterCard, MCI, Nabisco Foods, Pfizer, Republic National Bank.

133 East 36th Street
New York, NY 10016
212 889 9337
www.bfdg.com

Bernhardt Fudyma Design Group has long demonstrated how a sophisticated and successful graphic design firm can adapt to changing times, fashion and design whimsy. Its approach is fundamental: move beyond superficially decorative design where words and art combine only in an aesthetic way. Take design to the next level. Create a conceptual platform for each assignment. Focus not on an idea but *the* idea, then create a visual vocabulary that enriches the overall communication. "We understand that design aesthetic relies on the deft use of composition, color, texture, and scale," says Janice Fudyma, "but we demand more of ourselves. Whether we work on a logo, marketing brochure or web site, our creative process requires a clear, conceptual vision." Such strong views have sharpened the firm's focus—and to the benefit of its clients. With 25 years of experience and perspective, Bernhardt Fudyma foresees a future of continuing change, interesting challenges—and most importantly—great design.

above
Annual report for John Wiley and Sons, Inc., New York, NY. By juxtaposing images of both traditional and electronic publishing processes, a visual theme was created based upon Wiley's use of those complementary technologies. Designers, Iris Brown and Janice Fudyma; photography, David Arky.

below
Packaging for a training program by Learning International, Stamford, CT. The program included a redesign of its key product line, from participant modules and leaders guides to evaluation materials and other ancillary components. Designers, Iris Brown and Janice Fudyma.

right
Quarterly publication for employees of Nabisco Foods. The publication's purpose is to inform employees of all company activities, personnel achievements and innovations. Designers, Bernhardt Fudyma Design Group.

right
Brochure for AIG Financial Products, Stamford, CT. The Financial Products division of American International Group had developed a family of services to help protect producers and consumers of oil and gas from volatile price-swings. A series of illustrated case studies explained various financial hedging techniques. Designers, Craig Bernhardt and Frank Baseman; illustrator, Brian Cronin.

left
Logo for National Media Corporation, Philadelphia, PA. The N-M-and-C letters represent the transmission wave length and the orbiting satellite time the company controls. Designers, Craig Bernhardt and Ignacio Rodriguez.

right
Janice Fudyma and
Craig Bernhardt.
Photography,
Ray Charles White.

above and left
Commemorative calendar
for Nabisco Foods,
Parsippany, NJ, 200th
anniversary. The calendar
was created in a time-line
format that paralleled the
introduction of the company's products with key
historical events since
1792. It was distributed to
100-thousand employees,
suppliers and key commer-
cial buyers.
Designers, Craig Bernhardt,
Iris Brown, Janice Fudyma
and Jane Sobczak; cover
typography, Gerard Huerta.

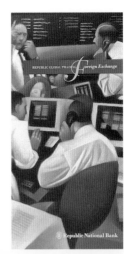

above and left
Marketing materials for Republic National Bank, New York, NY. The design unifies what was once unrelated brochures into a cohesive complement of materials that could be used in various combinations. A single, large panorama of the bank's trading room was created and engineered so that various segments of the activity could be isolated and used for the covers of the individual product brochures.
Designers, Craig Bernhardt, Janice Fudyma and Jennifer Markowitz; illustrator, Gary Kelly.

below
Residency recruiting materials for The Brooklyn Hospital Center, Brooklyn, NY. The recruiting materials were created so they could be assembled individually or in different clusters, which helped the hospital respond to specific requests from candidates interested in its various residency programs. Designers, Iris Brown, Janice Fudyma; photography, David Arky.

right and far right
Event materials for the Association on American Indian Affairs, New York, NY. A week-long event held at Lincoln Center promoting the work of contemporary Native American filmmakers. The organizers needed an overall identity and a complement of printed materials to raise funds, advertise and communicate to the participants and attendees of the various events. Designers, Craig Bernhardt and Iris Brown.

THE NATIVE AMERICAN FILM AND MEDIA CELEBRATION

left
Mutual funds materials for Bankers Trust, New York, NY. The bank had developed mutual funds to be made available to individuals through their company's retirement plans. Materials were produced that could outline 401K funds to financially astute corporate benefits managers who were the initial decision makers, but also explained the funds to the employee investors. Designers, Craig Bernhardt, Janice Fudyma and Jane Sobczak; illustrator, Douglas Smith.

right
Employee communication for Citibank, New York, NY. An annual review that reported on the performance of the various funds in the bank's savings incentive plan and, through the use of employee testimonials, presented the rationale for—and benefits of—investing in the plan. Designers, Craig Bernhardt and Iris Brown.

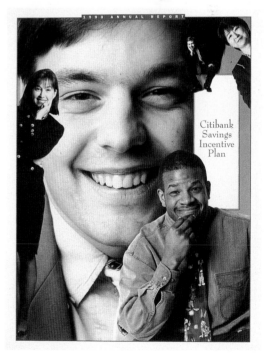

Blue Brick

Principals: Paul Krygowski,
Christopher Wise
Year Founded: 1990
Size of Firm: 5
Key Clients: AT&T,
Disney Online, Estee
Lauder, Harvard Business
School Press, HBO,
Letraset USA, Macy's,
Nickelodeon, *People*
Magazine, Philips Media,
Polygram, The Body Shop,
The Wool Bureau,
Warner Music.

131 Varick Street
Suite 913
New York, NY 10013
212 982 3880
www.bluebrick.com

lue Brick's goal is to produce work that is inspired and original. Regardless of the medium, Blue Brick doesn't settle for the predetermined or the expected. The company collaborates with like-minded clients to create design solutions that are a synthesis of innovation, revelation and communication—from placing a logo on a 6-foot high orange wig to including "20 Pairs of Galoshes" among 1400 photographs in a new stock photography product. Rejecting obvious solutions has led to new opportunities in other media where the company has created videos, interactive presentations and Internet sites that defy the commonplace.

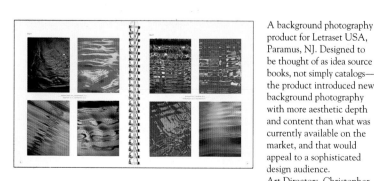

A background photography product for Letraset USA, Paramus, NJ. Designed to be thought of as idea source books, not simply catalogs— the product introduced new background photography with more aesthetic depth and content than what was currently available on the market, and that would appeal to a sophisticated design audience.
Art Directors, Christopher Wise and Paul Krygowski; designers, Wise, Akiva Boker and Sayuri Shoji; photography, Christopher Gallo.

left
From left: Christopher Wise
and Paul Krygowski.
Photography,
Ray Charles White.

left and above
Phototone CD set for
Letraset USA. The product
introduces Phototone on
CD-ROM. Blue Brick
packaged an off-the-shelf
CD case in a box with a
"dynamic" layered design to
show off the design possibilities of the product. Above
is a print ad for the product,
which shows backgrounds
in a creative combination.
Art Directors, Christopher
Wise and Akiva Boker;
designer, Boker; photography, Christopher Gallo.

bottom left
Phototone "Alphabets"
cover and spread. This is a
stock photography product
of unusual letters, numbers
and punctuation. The
brochure, a browsing catalog,
also illustrates the possible
usages of the letterforms,
which accompanies the
CD-ROM. The images can
be used as typography, stock
photography or backgrounds.
Art Director, Christopher
Wise; designers, Wise and
Akiva Boker.

Direct mail brochure, shopping bag and hang tag for The Wool Bureau, New York, NY. The project promotes the use of wool in casual mens wear. "Wool is consistently used in mens suits, but had not been considered a material suitable for casual clothing. The brochure was directed at designers and manufacturers to make them reconsider the possibilities of using wool in their products." The uncoated textured paper and the colors used throughout the design reflect a casual feeling and the copy has a witty, informal way of introducing the garments. Art Director, designer and copy, Christopher Wise; photography, Douglas Keeve.

The series of self-promotional postcards shown throughout the next four pages were made for current and potential clients. "We created what we hoped would be memorable images that would describe us as designers. A designer (now creative director of Nickelodeon), kept one of our cards for three years until he was in a position to hire us." Art Directors, Christopher Wise, Paul Krygowski and Akiva Boker; designers, Wise and Boker.

below left

Audio-visual package of business management theories for Harvard Business School Press, Cambridge, MA. The product, targeted for an executive/corporate audience, consists of a 28-page journal and three VHS tapes encased in Plexi-glass. The Harvard Press wanted to change their image with the design of this title, which incidentally became their best-seller. "No more leather embossed designs," they said. The design uses the cover of the journals to interact with the silk screened art on the front of the Plexi-glass case. Art Director, Christopher Wise; designers, Wise and Jin Pak; case design, Basi Cascella of Harvard Business School Press; photography, Christopher Gallo.

below right

Newsletter for Philips Media, New York, NY. The company wanted to present its corporate news using the hi-tech "buzz" associated with their most visible product—CD-interactive. The layout and colors change each month, giving the design a fluid "interactive edge." Art Director, Christopher Wise; designers, Wise and Terry Kardamakis.

 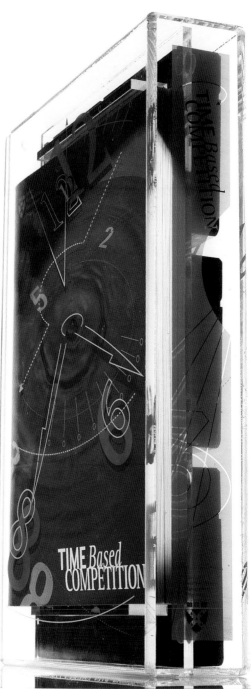

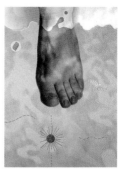

above
Product display for an eyewear licensee for Nickelodeon, New York, NY. The product stands out in the opticians environment and presents the glasses as stylish without being overtly fashion conscious. The "realistic, good-looking kids" were given wild, die-cut hair styles.
Art Directors, Christopher Wise and Paul Krygowski; designer, Wise; photography, Christopher Gallo.

right
Trade ads promoting Nicktoons for Nickelodeon. The ad tells the success story of Nicktoons to the animation and entertainment community. A sidebar presents Nicktoons facts, while the headline and characters support the main message that Nicktoons gives animators creative freedom. Creative Director, Christopher Wise and John Young; art director, Wise; copy, Young.

above
Self-promotional postcards.

opposite page left
"Opera," a 15-second on-air identity spot for Nickelodeon. The objective was to show off a new on-air look and grab kids' attention. "The Nickelodeon logo has to appear in an orange shape—so we gave new meaning to big hair." Creative Directors, Christopher Wise, Paul Krygowski and Akiva Boker; film direction, Krygowski and Wise; wig maker, Martin Izquierdo.

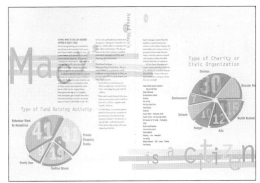

Redesign of an in-house magazine, STAR, for Macy's, New York, NY. The design is a hybrid of a magazine, newsletter and brochure. By avoiding a pre-determined form, each issue varies from the last. Creative Directors, Christopher Wise, and Christine Carter of Macy's; art director, Wise; designers, Wise and Terry Kardamakis.

Calori & Vanden-Eynden, Ltd.

Principals: Chris Calori, David Vanden-Eynden
Year Founded: 1981
Size of Firm: 5
Key Clients: ABC Broadcasting, Barneys New York, Corning, Inc., Hudson River Park Conservancy, Kohn Pedersen Fox Associates Architects, Michael Graves Architect, New Jersey Transit, New York City Transit Authority, Polshek and Partners Architects, Rockefeller Center Development Corporation, The Port Authority of New York and New Jersey, Thomson Consumer Electronics.

130 West 25th Street
New York, NY 10001
212 929 6302

B L A C K
H O U N D

above
Identity for Black Hound, a chic purveyor of chocolate truffles and baked goods in New York and New Jersey. Designers, Chris Calori and Julie Vogel.

alori and Vanden-Eynden is frequently asked, "Hey, are you guys in a band?" This question appropriately describes the spirit of this multi-disciplinary design office. It refuses to be pinned down to any dogmatic graphic style, any single project type, or anything else that could limit its love for design and the creative challenges of the design process. Diversity is the key word for the firm's design approach, with strong intellectual and pragmatic underpinnings. Calori & Vanden-Eynden's practice is grounded in the philosophy that design is a creative, problem-solving process, and that no two problems, or solutions, are the same. The firm embraces a wide range of graphic programs, including signage systems, identity development, and marketing and informational literature for a variety of distinguished clients. The result is internationally-recognized, award-winning design. Design that is distinguished by its broad, stylistic range—from traditional to hip, from seriously modernist to downright playful. Design that is elegantly resolved and appropriate to its context. In other words, design that is successful. What more would you want, besides groupies?

above
Highway entrance for the International Trade Center, Mt. Olive, NJ. The 30-foot-wide Verde marble and stainless steel monument forms a gateway for one of New Jersey's premier corporate parks. The project also encompassed signage master-planning, design and policy formulation for all signs within the 650-acre site. Designer, Chris Calori.

BRIGITTE'S BROWNIES

left
Logotype for the upscale bakery, Brigitte's Brownies, Doylestown, PA. The identity is also applied to product labels, packaging and the stationery system. Designers, Chris Calori and Gina De Benedittis.

left
David Vanden-Eynden and Chris Calori: Stylish, confident, and blonde. Photography, Ray Charles White.

below left
Signage for the Tribeca Bridge, New York, NY. Sculptured stainless steel letters with contrasting finishes create a monumental statement for the bridge's entrance.

below center
Highly-detailed curved stainless steel signs at the bridge's landing reinforce its machine-age style. Designers, Chris Calori and Bob Henry.

below right
A series of real estate leasing promotions made for a diverse collection of buildings under the management of Williamson, Picket, Gross, Inc., New York, NY. Designer, Chris Calori

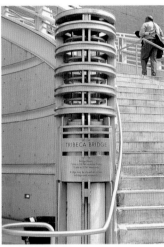

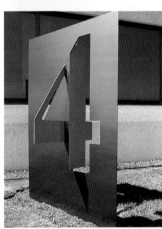

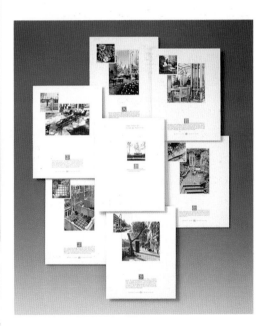

far left and left
Signage system for Royal Executive Park, Town of Rye, NY. Rigid metal banners feature heraldic shield images and bright colors. Identification sculptures help visitors to distinguish between six similar-looking buildings. Designers, David Vanden-Eynden and Julie Vogel.

above
Promotional brochure for Signe Nielsen Landscape Architecture, New York, NY. The brochure is quiet in nature, elegant and professional. Designers, David Vanden-Eynden and Julie Vogel.

Architectural signage pro-
gram for the Rock and Roll
Hall of Fame and Museum,
Cleveland, OH; designed
to reflect the building's
modernist architectural style.
Designers, David Albertson,
Chris Calori, Alexander
Isley and David Vanden-
Eynden. Created in associ-
ation with Alexander Isley
Design, Redding, CT.

above
Entry plaza monument sign
for the ultimate shrine of
rockdom.

right
Building directories provide
clear information for disori-
ented rock fans.

far right
Electric-blue neon signs
enhance the stage-like
quality of the building's
main lobby.

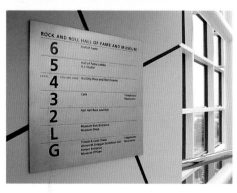

right
Logotype for Woodrow's
Bar & Restaurant,
Princeton, NJ, a "yuppie
fern bar" in Woodrow
Wilson's college town.
Designers, Chris Calori,
Julie Vogel and Kevin Yates.

left and below
Signage system for
Inventure Place/The
National Inventors Hall
of Fame, Akron, OH. Bright
colors and careful detailing
allow signs to stand out
while integrating with the
architecture. The logotype
plays on the questions and
answers related to the
process of invention.

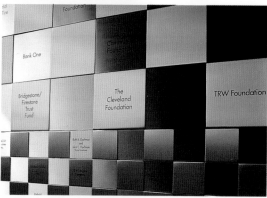

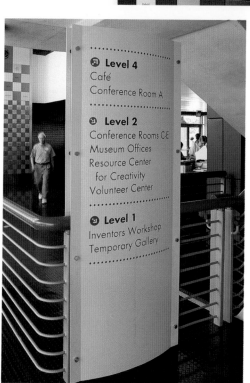

above
Detail of the stainless steel
donor recognition wall in
Inventure Place.

left
Bright yellow signs provide
information in a "can't-miss"
manner. The donor recog-
nition wall is visible in the
background.

right
The entry plaza's 80-foot-tall
signage tower.
Designers, David Vanden-
Eynden and Gina
De Benedittis.

Hudson River Waterfront Walkway

Map and Guide

Hudson River Waterfront Walkway

Hudson River Waterfront Walkway

Map Legend

HRWC
HUDSON RIVER WATERFRONT CONSERVANCY

left and above
Promotional materials and logotype for the Hudson River Waterfront Conservancy, Jersey City, NJ. The logotype utilizes a water theme, and a detailed map is on one side of the folding brochure. Designers, David Vanden-Eynden and Denise Funaro.

below
Symbol for Byelocorp, Inc., New York, NY, a company engaged in scientific, intellectual, and commercial exchange between Byelorussia and the United States. Designer, Chris Calori.

right
Signage program for the Valentine Riverside Museum, Richmond, VA. The program features bright red panels with triangular notches (the museum's color and logo) and yellow accents, forming a singular vocabulary to unify the various architectural styles of the 8-acre campus. Pictured on the far right is the site's main entrance monument. Twelve tons of Bluestone in a single piece, the monument features a natural cleft finish, hand carved letterforms, and a 700-pound red aluminum triangle. Designers, David Vanden-Eynden and Gina De Benedittis.

Pattern Building

← Valentine Riverside

Valentine Riverside

below
Signage and graphics for the Capital Cities/ABC Technical Services Building, New York, NY. The glass and neon reception desk sign provides a focal point for the main lobby. The graphics and mounting of all plaque signs reflect the asymmetry of the building's architecture. The main identification and address signs are integrated into the composition of the facade. Designers, David Vanden-Eynden and Ben Goodman.

right
Logotype for Mason Nielsen, PC, New York, NY, a landscape architecture and construction company. Designers, David Vanden-Eynden and Julie Vogel.

MASON · NIELSEN

left
Investment offering brochure for a REIT fund, Growth & Income Inc., Clifton, NJ. Designer, Chris Calori.

above left
Logotype for One Port Center, the headquarters building of the Delaware River Port Authority, Camden, NJ. Designers, Chris Calori and Gina De Benedittis.

above
Illuminated medallions identify the three towers of New York University's 800-student dormitory complex. The "pre-vandalized" door signs hide damage from keys and daily abuse. Designers, Chris Calori and Brenda Sisson.

Carin Goldberg Design

Principal: Carin Goldberg
Year Founded: 1982
Size of Firm: 2
Key Clients:
Doubleday, Grove/Atlantic,
Farrar, Straus & Giroux;
HarperCollins, Houghton
Mifflin, Hyperion Books,
Penguin USA, Random
House, Scribner, Simon &
Schuster, Warner Books,
William Morrow.

One University Place
New York, NY 10003
212 674 6424

 arin Goldberg's early career was marked with rigorous attention to sophisticated visual imagery as a designer in the golden years at CBS Records. Her skills were refined working in the subjective world of book jacket design. Goldberg displays an incredibly versatile sense of visual thinking, helping to reinvigorate the medium. Her intuitive savvy can be seen in the breath-taking single images, miniature posters that, as she says apologetically, often require creating something through found visual material. Though Goldberg is extremely grounded in the history and principles of design, she eschews formal theory and dogma. This humility is part of Goldberg's character. "Design, for me, is intuitive. The goal is to solve each problem intelligently, and hopefully at the same time, make it beautiful."

above
Book jacket design for *Bone*, by Faeng Myenne, Hyperion Books, New York, NY. The novel portrays a young Chinese-American woman growing up in the sometimes-sequestered community of San Francisco's Chinatown. It is a story of the sorrow and frustration of her immigrant family and their struggles with assimilation and loss. Designer, Carin Goldberg; photography, Genthe.

right
Logo for Cultiva, a new skin moisturizer, New York, NY. The product is made with herbal ingredients and added sunscreen. Designer, Carin Goldberg; illustrator, Anthony Russo.

right
Carin Goldberg and Jake.
Photography,
Ray Charles White.

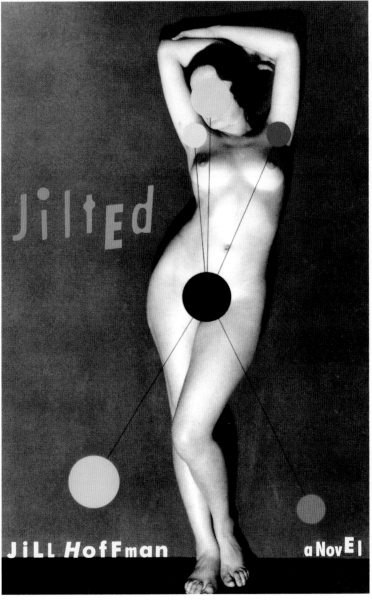

left
Logo for Vintage Books,
New York, NY. The logo is
a mark of identification for
Vintage Master Musicians,
a series of biographies about
musicians such as Beethoven,
Wagner, Mozart and Vivaldi.
Designer, Carin Goldberg.

above
Book jacket design for *Jilted*,
by Jill Hoffman, Simon &
Schuster, New York, NY.
The novel's main character
is a grown woman coming
of age and living in New
York as a poet.
Designer, Carin Goldberg;
photography, Man Ray.

above
Book jacket design for *Under
My Skin*, by Doris Lessing,
HarperCollins, New York,
NY. The first volume of her
memoirs covering the first
part of her life and work.
Designer, Carin Goldberg.

below
Book cover series for the complete catalog of Kurt Vonnegut's work (six out of 14 shown), Dell Publishing, New York, NY. Designer, Carin Goldberg; illustrator, Gene Greif.

opposite page right
Book jacket design for *The History of the Blues; the Roots, the Music, the People from Charley Patton to Robert Cray*, written by Francis Davis, Hyperion Books.

Designer, Carin Goldberg; jacket photo courtesy of Mimosa Records Production Inc.

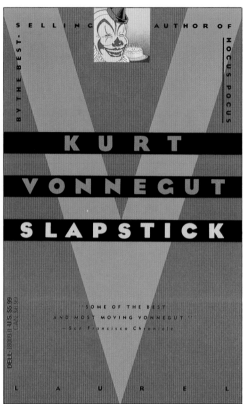

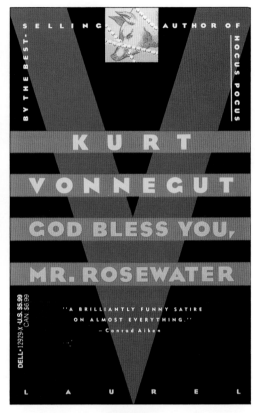

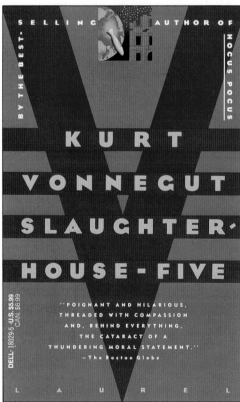

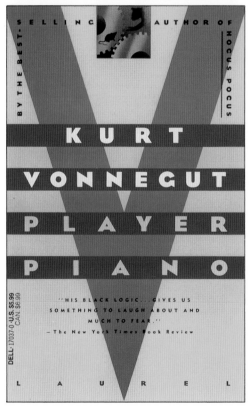

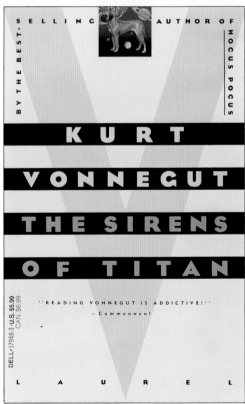

THE HISTORY OF THE BLUES THE ROOTS, THE MUSIC, THE PEOPLE FROM CHARLEY PATTON TO ROBERT CRAY FRANCIS DAVIS

far right
Book jacket design for *Measure for Measure*, by Tom Levenson, Simon & Schuster. The book is about the juxtapositions and over-lapping similarities in music and science. Designer, Carin Goldberg.

right
Book jacket design for *The Male Ego*, by Willard Gaylin, Ph.D, Penguin USA, New York, NY. Designer, Carin Goldberg

far right
Book jacket design for *Classic Crews*, a selection of essays by Harry Crews, Simon & Schuster. Designer, Carin Goldberg.

right
Book jacket design for *The Book of J*, Grove/Atlantic, New York, NY. Translated from Hebrew by David Rosenberg and interpreted by Harold Bloom. The authors recovered a lost masterpiece by a nameless writer known as "J," also the author of the oldest and most powerful stories in the bible. Designer, Carin Goldberg.

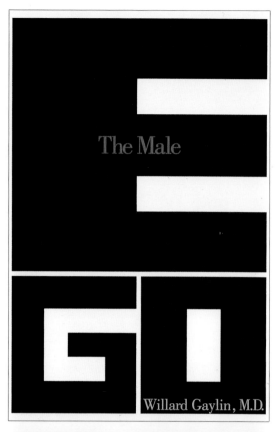

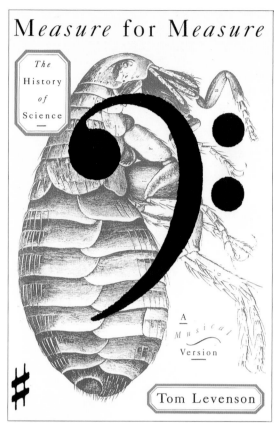

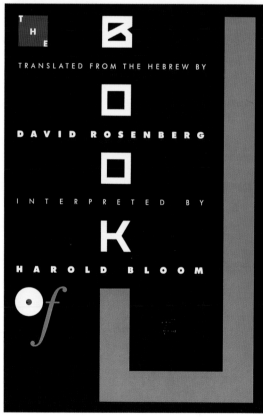

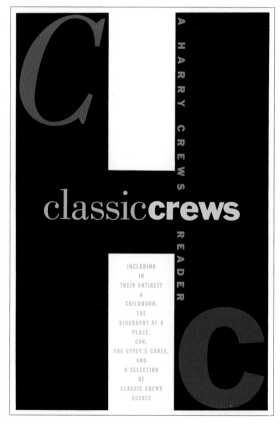

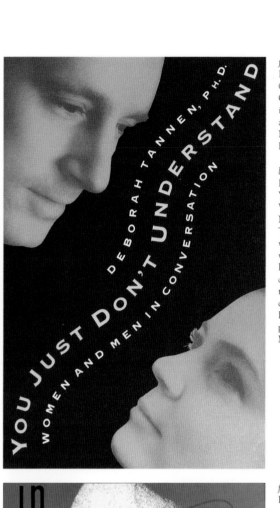

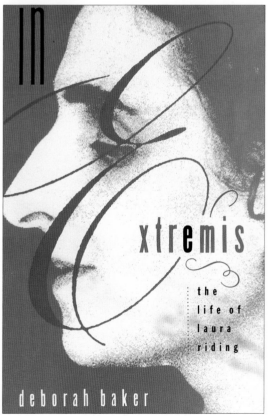

far left
Book jacket design for
Olga, by Fernando Morais,
Grove/Atlantic. The book
is a non-fictional account of
a woman who resisted the
Nazis during World War II.
Designer, Carin Goldberg.

left
Book jacket design for
You Just Don't Understand,
William Morrow, New York,
NY. Written by Deborah
Tannen, a sociolinguist
who, through understanding
women and men's style of
language, offer answers to
questions that confound
their attempts to communicate with each other.
Designer, Carin Goldberg;
photography,
Marcia Lippman.

far left
Book jacket design for *The
Queen's Throat*, by Wayne
Koestenbaum, Simon &
Schuster. The book is about
the long-observed affinity
that gay men have for opera,
and shows the complexities
of the threads that tie the
two together.
Designer, Carin Goldberg.

left
Book jacket design for *In
Extremis*, by Deborah Baker,
Grove/Atlantic.
Designer, Carin Goldberg.

Carla Hall Design Group, Inc.

Principal: Carla Hall
Year Founded: 1980
Size of Firm: 8
Key Clients: J.P. Morgan
Investment Management,
Oppenheimer Fund
Management, Shattuck
Hammond Partners,
UAM Retirement Plan
Services, Sentinel Financial
Services Company,
Showtime Networks, SkyTel,
The University Club,
The Vanguard Group,
The Wyatt Company.

261 West 85th Street
New York, NY 10024
212 799 4850
www.chdg.com

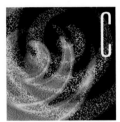

Carla Hall Design Group, a visual marketing firm, is dedicated to supporting its clients' business goals. Creative sensibility and leadership have earned Hall and her staff a reputation for excellence and innovation. Inside a framework of strategic thinking, the firm concentrates on corporate identity and collateral programs, annual reports, three dimensional design and on-line presentations. "Your aid in evolving our identity system, capabilities brochure and business development plan was outstanding. The design concepts you proposed were always market-focused and their execution was meticulous with a constant eye on quality and cost," said Joe Tarella of Greenfield. Sawicki. Tarella., Architects. It is that dedication and creativity that fosters the firm's long-term client relationships and has resulted in many prestigious design and business awards.

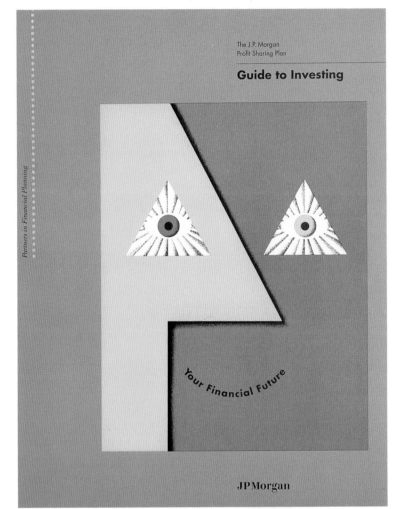

top
Handbook design for J.P. Morgan, New York, NY. The Guide to Investing educated company employees about investing for retirement. Compelling illustrations were used on posters, brochures and videos, and set a new graphic direction within the company's Human Resources department. Designers, Carla Hall and James Keller; illustrator, Terry Allen.

right
Winning Investment Strategies, an annual report for Alliance Capital Management L.P., New York, NY. Selected from the Chairman's art collection, 20th-century prints of team sports expressed the company's agility, strength, and adaptability. The design won the 1994 ARC Award of Merit. Designers, Carla Hall and James Keller.

left
Carla Hall in her studio.
Photography,
Ray Charles White.

Generic Employee
Investment Kit for J.P.
Morgan Investment
Management, New York,
NY. An illustrated character
searches for his investment
options, providing a humorous theme for the series that
includes a 20-page handbook,
10 color-coded mutual fund
brochures, a phone card,
sales sheets with templates,
folder and an envelope.
Designers, Carla Hall and
James Keller; illustrator,
Frank Ansley.

Diversify for a more fruitful portfolio.

4 Select specific plan investment options.

Now you are ready to actually build your portfolio. Certainly, there is a lot to think about — your individual **needs**, what those needs mean in terms of investment **return**, how much **time** you have to reach those goals, and what **investments** you will use to reach them.

Proctor & Gamble and J.P. Morgan Investment will supply information about the specific investments that are available through your Plan. Read this

information carefully — it's important that you understand what each option seeks to achieve and what investments it relies on to do so.

Through The P&G Subsidiaries Savings Plans, you have a valuable opportunity to really make a difference in the kind of financial future you'll have. Take advantage of it. Your financial future is too important to take for granted.

When picking investments...

Think about *diversification* — spread your money out to reduce risk. Emphasize those investments that

have the best chance of meeting your goals. And, remember that your decisions aren't set in stone —

as your personal situation, prefer-ences or goals change, reevaluate your choices and adjust your mix.

22

23

opposite page
Publication for Skidmore Ownings & Merrill, New York, NY. Directed to specific market segments such as airport planning, health care and interiors, coordinated publications were designed to expand Skidmore's business. Designers, Carla Hall and James Keller; cover photo, Scott Barrow.

The Pierpont Bond Fund

The Pierpont Diversified Fund

The JPM Institutional Money Market Fund

The JPM Institutional U.S. Small Company Fund

For the potential to earn higher income...

Don't put all your eggs in one basket...

When capital preservation is important...

For high total return potential.

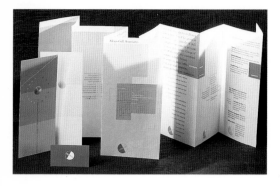

left
Corporate identity and brochure for Alexis Gill, White Plains, NY. Vellum translucent paper, and unusual color palette, format and typography were used to attract institutional clients interested in management training services and products, and to differentiate the company's position. Designers, Carla Hall and James Keller; illustrator, Keller.

REGIS

left
Corporate identity, marketing, and educational materials for Regis Retirement Plan Services, New York, NY. The program includes stationery, a capabilities brochure, and an enrollment kit with a 16-page, four-color Guide to Investing. The system won the 1995 Champion International Imagination Award, and first place at the International Association of Business Communicators, New York ACE competition. Designers, Carla Hall and Brian Jacobs; illustrator, Richard Goldberg.

left
Capital campaign brochure
for Audrey Cohen College,
New York, NY. Time
lines, case studies and
iconography create a
cohesive identity profiling
all aspects of the college.
Designers, Carla Hall,
James Keller and Brian
Jacobs; illustrator, Jacobs.

above
Corporate identity and
annual report for Shattuck
Hammond Partners, New
York, NY, an investment
banking company that serves
the health care industry.
Because the competition's
"distinctly conservative"
image, bright colors, textured
paper, and bold photography
were used to distinguish and
introduce the company and
its national clients.
Designers, Carla Hall and
Brian Jacobs; photography,
Lonnie Kalfus, Scott Barrow.

below
Brochure for Discovery
Partners, New York, NY.
Created to attract high net-
worth investors, it needed
to inspire trust in the four
managers and make their
"buy" and "sell" process clear.
Designers, Carla Hall and
James Keller; illustrator,
Dan Baxter; photography,
David Pollack.

above and right
Capabilities brochure for
KPMG Peat Marwick,
Washington D.C. Details
from the cover illustration
express key concepts of
partnership, customer service
and state-of-the-art services.
Captions are treated as
"stream-of-conscious" visuals.
Designers, Carla Hall and
James Keller; illustrator,
John Mattos.

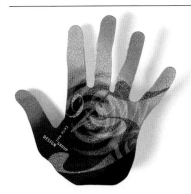

left
Self-promotional program. Every year the firm's clients get a "present" that doubles as the annual identity for the firm. The current theme is Hands-On "because we are a hands-on, client-responsive firm," says Hall. The previous years' promotions were various collectible buttons (opposite page). Designers, Carla Hall Design Group; illustrators, Brian Jacobs and James Keller.

above and right
Newsletter and corporate capabilities brochure for REBO Studio, New York, NY. Bold colors and typography express the firm's mission, "Changing the way the world sees." Designers, Carla Hall, James Keller and Brian Jacobs; illustrator, Jacobs.

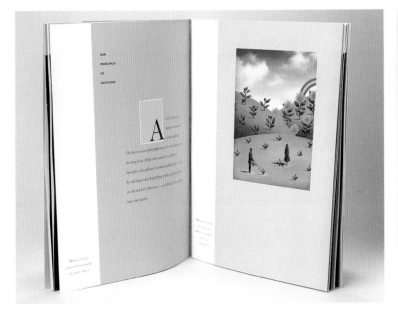

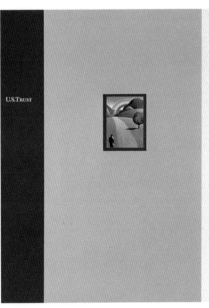

left
Brochure for U.S. Trust Company of New York, NY. Six paintings expressed the relationship between the bank and their clients and enabled the reader to understand the services and philosophy. Designers, Carla Hall and James Keller; illustrator, George Abe.

mev

M   U

THE UNVERIFIABLE NOTION OF GRACE

Myth

Looking for movement in shadow;

VS

V S

S E

the power of an empty chamber.

Book

Photography: Wout DeVringer, Faydherbe & DeVringer, Den Haag · Kiss by Frank Gargiulo · Concept and Inspiration: Myth & Book, Bates Hon, New York.

Chermayeff & Geismar Inc.

Principals: Ivan Chermayeff, Tom Geismar, John Grady, Steff Geissbuhler
Year Founded: 1960
Size of Firm: 35
Key Clients: Bronx Zoo, Conservation Trust of Puerto Rico, Crane & Co., Edward S. Gordon Company, FactSet Research Systems, Gemini Consulting, Harry S. Truman Library, May Department Stores, Mobil Corporation, Monadnock Paper Mills, National Building Museum, New York Public Library.

15 East 26th St.
12th Floor
New York, NY 10010
212 532 4499

hermayeff & Geismar Inc. continues a long and enviable tradition of diversity in its design practice. Founded in 1960 by Ivan Chermayeff and Tom Geismar, the firm quickly emerged as one of New York's first cross disciplinary studios, collaborating directly with leaders in business, government and cultural institutions. Joined by Steff Geissbuhler and the architect John Grady in the early seventies, the principals broadened the scope of their work to include two and three-dimensional design that often blends graphic, interior and exhibition design into one project. In the wake of Chermayeff & Geismar's early success with the highly publicized logo and identity system for Mobil Oil, the firm has continued to create many of the world's most identifiable visual symbols for companies such as NBC, Time Warner, HarperCollins, Merck, and Viacom. Early exhibition work in world fairs and traveling shows has been followed by many memorable interpretive exhibits in history and science museums. The Smithsonian Institution's "A Nation of Nations" exhibit was considered a landmark in visual storytelling. The more recent Statue of Liberty exhibit and Ellis Island Immigration Museum exemplify the continuation of that standard. Through the ongoing excellence and variety of its work, Chermayeff & Geismar Inc. has altered the practice of graphic design and changed the way designers are perceived in America and abroad.

above
One of a series of catalogs for Knoll. The piece conveys the mix and match quality of their interactive line of components.

below
Reference booklet for Crane & Co. Business Papers, Dalton, MA. The booklet gives international standards for stationery formats, measurements, codes and conversions.

right
Identification for the lower
Manhattan Business
Improvement District,
New York, NY.

far right
Logotype and identity
program for The Hillier
Group, Princeton, NJ, a
major architecture, interior
design and engineering firm.

right
A series of ads and posters
for Gemini Consulting,
Morristown, NJ, featuring
provocative quotes.

below
Series of booklets about a
variety of printing processes,
pre-press issues and on-press
techniques for Monadnock
Paper Mills, Bennington, NH.

"We are what we
repeatedly do.
Excellence, then,
is not an act,
but a habit." Aristo

GEMINI

Gemini Consulting.
Worldwide Leaders in
Business Transformation."

"The measure of
success is not
whether you have
a tough problem
to deal with,
but whether it's the
same problem you had
last year." John Foster Dulles

GEMINI

Gemini Consulting.
Worldwide Leaders in
Business Transformation."

"By the time
the rules of the game
are clear,
the windows of
opportunity will have
closed." Santhanam C. Shekar

GEMINI

Gemini Consulting.
Worldwide Leaders in
Business Transformation."

above
Identification for a visitor's center for the Heritage Trails in downtown New York City. The program included color-coded street markers for walking tours that lead visitors to sites and attractions of historic New York.

below
Press kit, fundraising brochure and identity for The New Victory Theater, New York, NY. The symbol and identity was created in collaboration with a group of teenagers. The theater is non-profit for the city's youth.

top left
Symbol for Big Apple Circus, New York, NY. A new tent, posters, an alphabet and several circus-icon characters were developed for marketing and merchandising.

left
Identification program and on-air graphics for Torneos y Competencias, a major sports television programming group in Buenos Aires, Argentina. The still frames are from two different animated on-air signatures.

below
Identification program for National Public Radio, Washington D.C. The soundwave initials are designed as tiles and are used in various configurations.

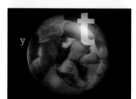

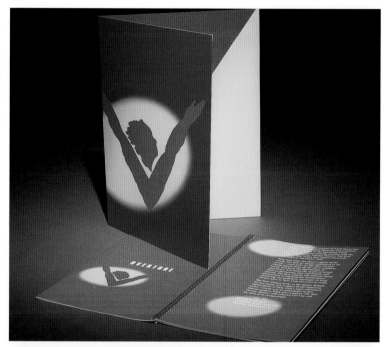

above
Promotional logotype, identification program and centennial graphics for New York Public Library, including its four research and 82 branch libraries. The letterforms depict the multitude of information media contained in the collections—from print and pictorial to Braille and digital.

left
Identification program and on-air graphics for Sony Entertainment Television, a new network presently broadcasting in India and throughout South America.

right
Poster that is part of a campaign to introduce a new line of Knoll office seating. Cloud imagery and soft type were chosen to emphasize the comfort quality achieved through ergonomics testing.

below
Series of promotional brochures for a major New York metropolitan area real estate firm, the Edward S. Gordon Company. Each brochure briefly conveys the firm's expertise in a targeted area of business.

Knoll Parachute

right
Identity, logotype, entrance sculptures, interior and environmental graphics and gambling materials for New York State's first casino for the Oneida Indian Nation, located in Verona, NY.

To explain science and nature to younger audiences, complicated issues of global importance need to be summed up compellingly and simply. Hands-on experience invites participation by people of all ages. Interactive technologies help to shed light on the complexities in the world. These five exhibits are designed primarily for young urban children and their families.

right
In New York City's Van Cortlandt Park's Urban Ecology Center, a lively grid of touchable, natural materials, push-button puzzles, and hunt-and-seek collages of leaves and insect helps to familiarize visitors of all ages with the wonder of the park outside.

above
At Kidpower, the science playground of the New York Hall of Science in Queens, a huge, colorful metal armature of catwalks, tubes and slides holds dozens of energetic exhibits that allow young visitors to experience physics.

left and above
Science City brings the New York Hall of Science to the streets. Bold and colorful demonstrations attract passers-by to pause and learn about the science and technology that make cities work.

left and below
Up in the Urban Treehouse at the Children's Museum of Manhattan's garden, kids are invited to climb, pull, crank and dig. They encounter urban environmental issues as they participate, and learn to "Reduce, Reuse and Recycle."

far left and left
Inside the Bronx Zoo's World of Birds, architectural barriers between visitors and bird habitats were minimized. Overhead graphics and engaging technology focus the visitor's attention on principles of ecology and the hazards of human intervention.

Desgrippes Gobé & Associates

Principals: Marc Gobé
(New York) and Joël
Desgrippes (Paris)
Year Founded: 1970, Paris
1985, New York
Size of Firm: 80, New York
Key Clients:
Ann Taylor, The Albertville
Olympic Games, Brooks
Brothers, Cartier, FILA
Sport, IBM, The Limited,
Inc., Rockport, SNCF,
Godiva, Mark Cross,
The Coca-Cola Company,
Liz Claiborne, Rollerblade,
Ralph Lauren, Sears,
Victoria's Secret.

411 Lafayette Street
New York, NY 10003
212 979 8900
www.dga.com

Desgrippes Gobé—one of the top ten design groups worldwide—is a full-service marketing and design consultancy specializing in image management and strategic design. The firm's integrated approach to brand building results in the ultimate objective: brand presence. "To create the most powerful brands, every aspect of a company needs to send a consistent message," says Marc Gobé, CEO and executive creative director. "That means addressing the corporate identity, packaging, signage, retail and interactive environments in which the product communicates and is sold." With offices in New York, Paris, Tokyo and Seoul, the group's mission is to develop retail and consumer brands that evoke an emotional response in the consumer worldwide. This is achieved through a proprietary visual research methodology called SENSE®. An acronym for Sensory Exploration plus Need States Evaluation, SENSE® analyzes a brand's visual equities and targets the codes and cues that speak to a consumer's tastes and values, thereby evoking loyalty between a product or service and its target customer. "In today's complex global market, companies of all sizes are finding that effective brand building that sends a relevant message to the consumer is a vital marketing tool for keeping an edge over the competition." And for extolling the virtues of good design.

Retail presence program that allowed IBM to break through the cluttered electronics store environment. A "cybersky" graphic was created as a proprietary visual element to unify and link the IBM sub-brands together while additional elements allowed them to compete individually within their respective categories.

right
The Aptiva program speaks to consumers' values on an emotional level, inviting them to "Touch New Worlds."

left
Marc Gobé and Joël
Desgrippes.
Photography,
Ray Charles White.

right
Coca-Cola Olympic
City logo.

opposite page
ThinkPad communicates the core essence of its brand while sharing a corporate voice with the Aptiva line of personal computers. The compact, streamlined fixture sets a stage for the simple, sophisticated ergonomics of the ThinkPad computer.

Coca-Cola Company's integrated communications program for the 1996 Centennial Olympic Games in Atlanta, GA. Coca-Cola positioned itself as a brand that understood consumers as fans, and shared in their excitement for the Olympics. The resulting presence program ranged from packaging and advertising to merchandise, concession stands and the entire Coca-Cola Olympic City theme park. The park allowed fans to experience the games from the viewpoint of the athletes through the company's 15-acre interactive amusement park. The design strategy was to develop individual graphic "suites"—components of graphic elements, symbols, colors and icons that could be used individually or collectively to communicate the "For the Fans" positioning. The final packaging design tapped the nostalgia surrounding the soft drink's alliance with the games since 1928, and emphasized the theme of "refreshment."

52

MARK CROSS

NEW YORK

NEW YORK

right and above
Identity system to revitalize
the heritage of America's
oldest leather goods manufacturer, Mark Cross. The
two versions of the 150-
year-old crest were designed
with a custom typeface for
the wordmark to be com-
patible with it; both were
designed to be used together
or independently. A new
proprietary corporate color
palette and checkerboard
pattern were selected for
the packaging and carried
through into the store
design. The pattern picks
up on one of the brand's
unique aspects: its product
line of games such as chess,
backgammon and checkers.

right
All packaging is produced
using recycled paper;
antique bronze grommets
and custom-colored cord
for handles for the shopping
bag; ribbon is custom-dyed
and printed with metallic
bronze; and stock tissue
color is silkscreened with
the same color ink.

Identity and design for Ann Taylor's Madison Avenue flagship store, New York. In fitting with the established Ann Taylor market, the store design needed to be elegant, sophisticated and refined. The sales area covers four floors. The staircase became the ordering point within the floor plan for the layout of departments and fixtures. The staircase also provides immediate visual access from the entrance to the mezzanine level that has been entirely devoted to fragrance—the Destination

bath and home line packaging uses materials materials such as wood, cork, frosted glass and textured paper to reinforce its identity. Reusable packaging was selected to use wherever possible.

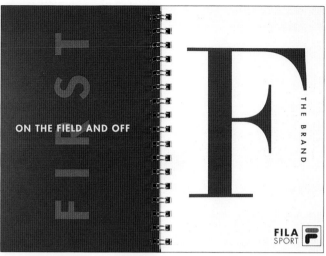

ON THE FIELD AND OFF

FIRST

F

THE BRAND

FILA SPORT

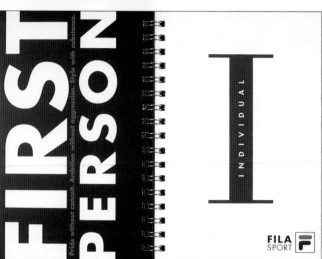

FIRST
PERSON

Pride without conceit. Ambition without aggression. Style with substance.

I

INDIVIDUAL

FILA SPORT

FILA SPORT

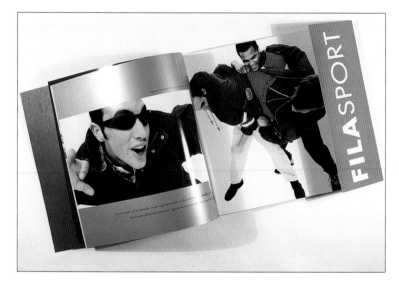

CHA
MPEI
ONS

ON THE FIELD

AND IN LIFE

LIFE STYLE

L

FILA SPORT

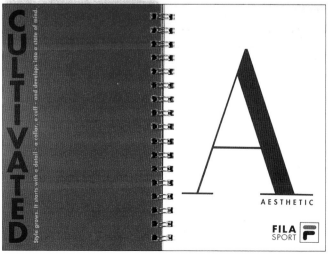

CULTIVATED

Style grows. It starts with a detail - a collar, a cuff - and develops into a state of mind.

A

AESTHETIC

FILA SPORT

Retail brand identity program including outdoor advertising for FILASport, New York, NY. To combine FILA's European craftsmanship with an active American lifestyle, the collection uses an advertising strategy that builds its reputation for performance gear worn and endorsed by professional athletes. The challenge was to establish a visual territory, and design a graphics program including a lifestyle/ garment presentation book and garment graphics that communicates the company's spirit.

opposite page/ right
The Gingham line of cologne, gel, lotion and bath crystals for Bath & Body Works. The simple blue-and-white pattern reflects the appeal of country living. The packaging for the foaming bath oil crystals was inspired by an old-fashioned milk bottle; the soap is embossed with a basket-weave pattern. These elements express the basic premise of Bath & Body Works: to offer a full collection of personal care products using only natural ingredients. A second scent, Heartland, continues the theme in a vibrant red color scheme.

below
Packaging for Victoria's Secret Encounter fragrance line utilizes pure geometric shapes, clean type and is packaged in a slick fushia wedge-shaped box for contrast.

right
Packaging for Victoria's Secret Vanille Essence de Voyage. Eight different vanilla-based scents were created to illustrate the concept of fragrances inspired by travel to exotic lands. Bamboo and grass motifs decorate the inside and out of the box and are rendered in frosted glass around the bottle.

above right and right
For its new perfume, Boucheron, Paris, chose the name Jaïpur, a mythical location where the most refined goldsmiths crafted lucky-charm bracelets for newlyweds. The bracelet bottle is the symbol of a century-old artisan know-how. It leads into a universe of luxury and femininity, which hovers between the worlds of the perfumer and the jeweller. In this line, the bottles combine polished glass, gold, and sapphire blue, the brand's signature color.

left
Web site created for Lancome that uses clutter-free, pop-up windows to communicate in-depth information. The site leverages an interest in Lancome products into an ongoing dialogue with customers by offering them relevant information while reinforcing its brand image. Designed to attract a younger consumer without alienating its existing clients, the site correlates to the fall 1996 advertising campaign and reflects the new "look" of Lancome.

Design/Writing/Research

Principals: J. Abbott Miller,
Ellen Lupton
Senior staff: Paul Carlos,
Luke Hayman, Jane Rosch
Year Founded: 1986
Size of Firm: 6
Key Clients: Geoffrey Beene,
Dance Ink Foundation,
Guggenheim Museum,
National Building Museum,
Vitra, *Grand Street*,
The Museum of Modern
Art, Davis Museum,
Columbia University,
Abrams Inc., M.I.T.

214 Sullivan Street
Sixth Floor
New York, NY 10012
212 228 6787
www.kiosksite.com

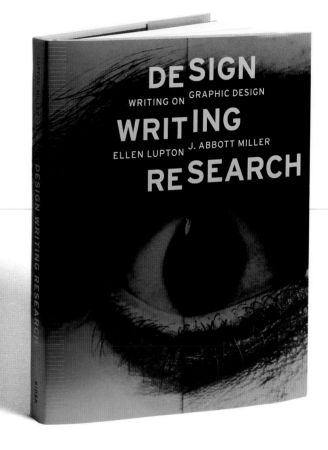

Design/Writing/Research combines the visual emphasis of a design studio with the conceptual and editorial rigor of writing, research, and content development. Founded in 1986 as an exploratory think-tank, the "design-writing-research" paradigm has evolved into a vital, multidisciplinary office. Not bound by any particular technology, medium or genre, the studio has created a niche for itself with visually dramatic and editorially ambitious projects, ranging from books and magazines, to identity projects, exhibitions, signage and multi-media work. The studio's work is rooted in the expressive potential of type to deliver visual and verbal messages with clarity, wit and drama.

The ABC's of ▲■●: *The Bauhaus and Design Theory*. The book explores the history and impact of this famous school of art and design. In print since its publication, its success has led to Spanish, German, and Korean-language editions. *Eye* magazine described it as a "model of the ways design and writing might be harnessed to probe and illuminate a visual subject."

Design Writing Research: Writing on Graphic Design features essays on theoretical and historical aspects of design. The book illuminates its wide-ranging subject by fusing form and content into an inventive and readerly ensemble. Topics range from the history of punctuation, the design of international pictures symbols, and the relationship of design to post-structuralism and semiotics.

Published in conjuntion with an exhibition at M.I.T., *The Bathroom, the Kitchen, and the Aesthetics of Waste*, looked at the development of household technologies. The exhibition and book brought this subject to life with humor and insight, mixing scholarship with an appreciation of popular culture.

The Bathroom
the Kitchen
and the Aesthetics of Waste

The "alphabet ruler" is an eloquent pun on the studio's hybrid activities of design, writing, and research. The ruler, which is the studio's trademark, is used on stationery and has also been produced as a limited edition multiple.

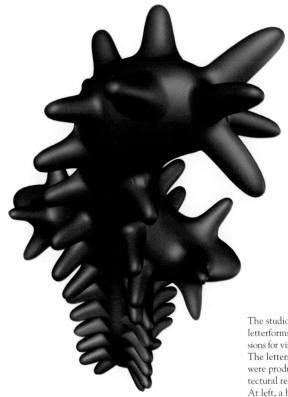

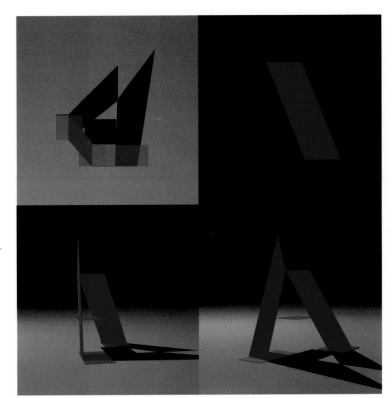

The studio has developed letterforms in three-dimensions for virtual environments. The letters represented here were produced with architectural rendering software. At left, a bulbous, pronged letter "f" as seen from an oblique angle; at right, a classical letter "A" rendered as a series of planes in space. These letters, and others, are published in a monograph called *Dimensional Typography*.

Printed Letters: The Natural History of Typography presented the history of type through the metaphor of natural history. The display cases were designed to echo the forms of the cases used for storing metal type specimens. Like natural history displays, the exhibition mixed man-made and natural curiosities.

DIAMANDA GALÁS

PLAGUE MASS *ILLUSTRATES THE SPECTATOR SPORT OF TORTURE. JUST AS ANCIENT ROMANS FLOCKED TO THE COLOSSEUM TO SEE PEOPLE TORTURED, AIDS HAS BECOME A SPECTATOR SPORT FOR MANY AMERICANS. THEY SEEM TO ENJOY WATCHING GAY MEN, PEOPLE OF COLOR, AND IV-DRUG USERS DIE.*

I SEE THE AIDS EPIDEMIC AS A KIND OF GERM WARFARE, AND ITS RESOLUTION HAS BEEN MANAGED THAT WAY, TOO. OTHERWISE IT WOULDN'T BE SO COMPLETELY OUT OF CONTROL. I CAN ALSO GUARANTEE THAT FOR EVERY REASON LIKE MYSELF WHO SAYS SOMETHING LIKE THIS, THERE ARE GOING TO BE NINETY-NINE OTHER PEOPLE WHO SAY, "CALM DOWN. THERE'S NO PROOF." WELL, THERE'S NO PROOF EITHER WAY. THEY HAVE NO MORE PROOF THAN I DO.

BILLIONS OF DOLLARS ARE SPENT ON MILITARY RESEARCH, BUT ONLY A FRACTION OF THAT AMOUNT IS PUT TOWARD EXISTING DISEASES IN THE POPULATION. IT'S NAIVE TO ASSUME THAT A LOT OF VIRUSES WE ARE NOW DEALING WITH HAVEN'T BEEN INTRODUCED BY CHANCE OR NEGLECT. SCIENCE INCLUDES BOTH. ◆ DIAMANDA GALÁS

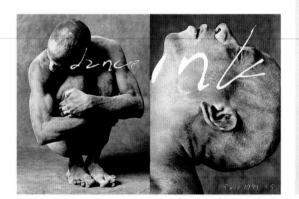

Dance Ink is a quarterly magazine devoted to dance and performance. Its strong and constantly changing visual persona has earned it many design awards, including four gold medals from the Society of Publication Designers, and three nominations from the National Magazine Awards. Hailed for its design as a "landmark" magazine, *Dance Ink* led to the publication of *Dancing on the Edge,* a book surveying the design and photography of *Dance Ink.*

pilar rioja

The Guggenheim Museum's magazine was designed to create a lively format for covering issues on contemporary art. A new font was created for it using Frank Lloyd Wright's distinctive lettering as a point of departure.

A number of posters designed for performing artists, including Philip Glass, Elizabeth Streb and Twyla Tharp.

Poster announcing a lecture series for the Princeton University School of Architecture. The open leaves of a book to suggest the volumetric shadow and light of architectural space.

World War II and the American Dream: How War Time Building Changed a Nation surveyed the impact of the war on architecture and industrial design. The exhibition at the National Building Museum in Washington D.C. consisted of photographs, models, and artifacts. Its design made dramatic use of large-scale photography to convey the immensity of the war effort. The entrance to the show was signalled by ten-foot-high painted letters.

fiberglass

vitra.
eames

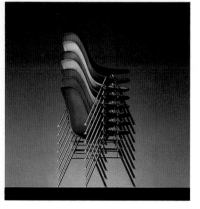

A tri-lingual catalog on the furniture of Charles and Ray Eames was written and designed for Vitra, a visionary, design-intensive company based in Switzerland. Vitra holds the license for producing Eames furniture in Europe and wanted a book that would reflect its committment to high craftsmanship. The catalog design sets out to honor the Eameses' work in contemporary terms, rather than mimicking their particular aesthetic.

The studio has worked on many projects with clothing designer Geoffrey Beene. The catalog *Geoffrey Beene 30* accompanied a museum retrospective on fashion designer Geoffrey Beene. With its technicolor imagery and pinking-sheared edges, the book's production parallels the elegance of its subject. Short texts on clothing by Franz Kafka are juxtaposed with the enigmatic expressions of models wearing the designer's clothing from the 1960s to the 1990s.

An exhibition at the Museum of the Fashion Institute of Technology in New York featured four large crisscrossing stairways that created a dramatic stage set for 30 years of the designer's clothing. A site-specific video was produced for projection onto a scrim: the effect was of a dancer ethereally moving from one end of the room to the other.

Geoffrey Beene is a definitive edition on the work of the acclaimed American designer. Conceived as an art book rather than a fashion catalogue, the book is a dramatic summation of the designer's career. Integrating work over a 30-year period, the book creates a strong narrative through the pacing and placement of images.

Diana DeLucia
Design, Ltd.

Principal: Diana DeLucia
Year Founded: 1985
Size of Firm: 9
Key Clients: American
Express, Citibank, Hyatt
Hotels, Krups, Kwasha
Lipton, Liz Claiborne,
MBNA America,
Mastercard, Medallion
Hotels, Inc.; NYL Care
Health Plan, New York Life
Insurance Co., Rockresorts,
Scholastic Inc.,
Swiss Bank Corporation.
853 Broadway

Suite 1605
New York, NY 10003
212 529 7600

Diana DeLucia has built a strong team that thrives on constantly being challenged. The importance of the client relationship is well understood and Diana Delucia's personal involvement on every project has been key to maintaining her client relationships dating back to the firm's opening in 1985. One of the policies is to have clients with diversity and work in disciplines that cut across the total communications spectrum. "We see diversity as a means to ensure freshness of ideas and to continuously challenge our varied interests," says DeLucia. Analyzing complex information—from the positioning of a bio-tech product in the development stage, to the launching of highly technical financial products in multiple markets—DeLucia Design has the ability to search beneath the obvious, to find meaning that appeals to the reader, and to illustrate it in a way that commands the attention of the audiences. The client roster not only includes Fortune 500 companies, but also boutique organizations in the financial, healthcare, travel and leisure industries. The firm's disciplines encompass direct mail, signage, annual reports, packaging, corporate and product identity, as well as electronic media.

above
Direct mail program targeting potential buyers of a new clothing line by Liz Claiborne Inc., New York, NY. Consumers received a packet of cards showing the fashions with text and icons explaining the products' features. The design challenge was making poor quality photographs look great. They were enhanced by changing the backgrounds and using hot colors to provide the most appealing contrast.
Design Director, Diana DeLucia; designers, Patricia Kovic and Sandra Monteparo.

below/opposite page
(left to right)
Self-promotional logo. Design Director, Diana DeLucia; designer, Shino Tanikawa.
Identity program for a luxury hotel in Hawaii, by Rockresorts, New York, NY. Design Director, Diana DeLucia; designer, Barbara Tanis.
Logo design for Arete Therapeutics, Los Angeles, CA, a bio-tech company researching central nervous system disorders. Design Director, Diana DeLucia; designer, John Farrar.

MANELE BAY

left
Identity development and card design for the national launch of an exclusive Platinum Plus Card, MBNA America Bank, NA, Wilmington, DE. Including marketing collateral and direct mail roll-out to over 20 million prospects, the program positions it as a premiere card, setting new standards of excellence in financial services. Design Directors, Diana DeLucia and Barbara Tanis; designers, John Farrar and Kai Zimmerman.

left
Promotional time management calendar for Innovation Printing and Lithography, Philadelphia, PA. Formatted as a desk piece with days displayed in a weekly format, a photographic tab system divides each month. The theme, "Time Management," was cleverly conveyed through the text that accompanied the photos. It included a yellow wood-grain pencil that matched the calendar's cover. Design Director, Diana DeLucia; designers, Barbara Tanis and Patricia Kovic.

below
Small budget identity and packaging program for Five Star Espresso, New York, NY, a coffee subscription program for lovers of Illy Cafe. The identity needed a light-hearted, not "over designed," approach. Subscribers receive a monthly newsletter with their coffee order, along with coffee cups, t-shirts and other premium items, all displaying the logo. Design Director, Diana DeLucia; designer, Frauke Ebinger.

ARETE THERAPEUTICS

right/opposite page
Self-promotional multimedia presentation for DeLucia Design. It introduces clients to multimedia capabilities. The six, key screen images are an interactive electronic presentation that is simple, yet inviting enough to attract a variety of audiences. Design Director, Diana DeLucia; designer, Frauke Ebinger.

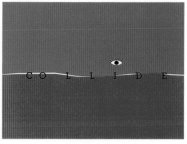

below/top row
Informational science brochure for Viagene, Inc., San Diego, CA. The brochure was targeted to potential investors and analysts. It explains Viagene's innovative gene transfer drugs. Stylized computer illustrations of cellular activity simplified explanations of complex processes. Design Director, Diana DeLucia; designer, Patricia Kovic.

below/bottom row
Brochure for Swiss Bank Corporation, New York, NY. Produced for the American market, the brochure promotes private banking services to high-net worth individuals; focusing on the personal attention to its client and the Swiss tradition of attention to detail. Design Director, Diana DeLucia; creative director, Albert Leutwyler; designer, Frauke Ebinger.

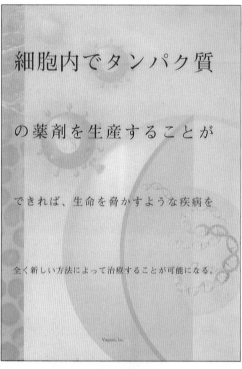

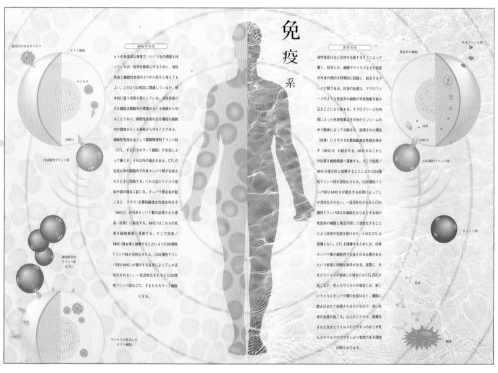

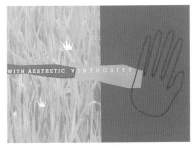

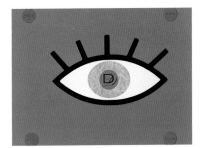

below/top row
Product catalog for Krups
North America, New York,
NY. The catalog needed to
visually unify 150 existing
product photographs that
were all shot on different
backgrounds, plus photo-
graph 40 new products.
Sections were created by
adding color over what
already existed, enhanced
by dramatic and colorful
still life photography of
associated images.
Design Director,

Diana DeLucia; designer,
Frauke Ebinger.

below/bottom row
Annual report for
Advacare Inc.,
Philadelphia, PA. The firm
provides administrative and
medical reimbursement
management to health care
providers. The report needed to visually depict a company that virtually had no
tangible product. The use
of a photographic perspec-

tive translated the compa-
ny's services into graphic
icons, creating a visually
compelling piece.
Design Director,
Diana DeLucia; designers,
Patricia Kovic and
Sandra Monteparo.

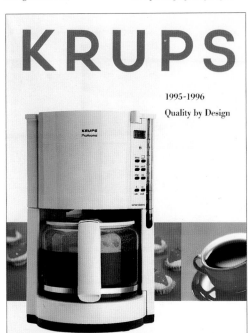

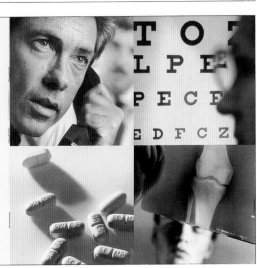

WATERMARK

WINGS

*m*edalist *inn*

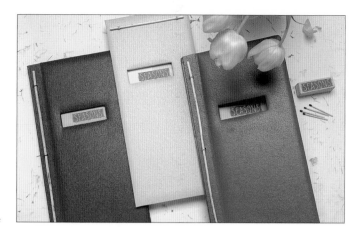

left
(from top)
Naming and identity program for Watermark Inc., New York, NY, a hotel management group. Design Director, Diana DeLucia; designer, Shino Tanikawa. Identity program for an exclusive travel company, Wings Private Travel Services, New York, NY. Design Director, Diana DeLucia; designer, John Farrar.

Identity program for a "limited services" group of hotels, Medalist Inns, Oklahoma City, OK. Design Director, Diana DeLucia; designers, Frauke Ebinger and Barbara Tanis.

right
Logo and menu design for Seasons Restaurant, Dallas, TX. The restaurant needed a name before an identity. "Seasons" was a natural—the menu is based on seasonal ingredients. The three meal menu-covers are color-coded with different handmade paper treatment on the interior. Design Director, Diana DeLucia; designer, John Farrar.

right
Hanbury Manor identity for Rockresorts, New York, NY. A 17th-century Jacobean Manor house transformed into a luxury hotel and resort in the countryside outside of London. The identity was designed to indicate the original time period. All printed materials were embossed or engraved, exclusive fabrics were used, and the logo was created as a mosaic at the bottom of the swimming pool. Design Director, Diana DeLucia; designer, Barbara Tanis.

Image and identity system for Medallion Hotels, Inc., New York, NY, a group of hotels appealing to upscale business travelers. Seven hotels exist in various cities, so the program needed the flexibility to adapt to different styles of architecture, geographic locations, as well as a myriad of printed and three-dimensional applications.
Design Director,
Diana DeLucia; designer,
Barbara Tanis.

Donovan and Green

Principals: Michael Donovan, Nancye Green
Year Founded: 1974
Size of Firm: 45
Key Clients: American Express, Celebrity Cruises, Citibank, F. Hoffmann-LaRoche, Hallmark, Liberty Science Center, Metropolitan Transit Authority, Ronald Reagan Presidential Foundation, Sony, Texas Instruments, Wilkhahn, 3M.

71 Fifth Avenue
New York, NY 10003
212 989 4050

Donovan and Green is a company dedicated to creating highly integrated solutions to an array of communications problems. Michael Donovan and Nancye Green have spent the past 20 years building the firm, which today comprises a core staff of 45, representing a diverse mix of talent and experience. Whether the goal is to educate, inform, entertain or sell, this multidisciplined firm crafts the process that leads to new understanding, new programs and new ways of communicating. The projects included here are evidence of broader experiences, each with a specific set of expectations—an information architecture that enables experts to communicate, an information environment that helps visitors learn, and naming and identity assignments that result in the creation and execution of new places and products.

left and below
Catalog for Sony Corporation, Park Ridge, NJ. Evaluation and redesign of Sony's existing premiums/wearables program include a strategic approach for enhancing and expanding it. The designers sourced merchandise, created product identification, and produced a catalog that became the foundation for the program's evolution. Project team: Nancye Green, Marge Levin, Vanessa Ryan and Allen Wilpon; photography, Amos Chan.

left
Product naming and identity for Sony Electronics, Park Ridge, NJ. The firm named and developed an identity for MagicLink, Sony's new "personal intelligent communicator" product. The name and logo infused the device with a personality while being suggestive of its key qualities— namely instant access to information through the use of interactive personal communications such as e-mail, faxing and paging. Project team: Nancye Green and Clint Morgan.

above
Institutional identity and public space development for the California Museum of Science and Industry, Los Angeles, CA. A concept and design for a new identity program was created for the institution as it positioned itself as a science-education center for the 21st century. Project team: Nancye Green, Clint Morgan, Susan Myers and Brian Stanlake.

left
Seated: Michael Donovan
and Nancye Green.
Partners, from left to right:
Susan Berman, Susan Myers
and Marge Levin.

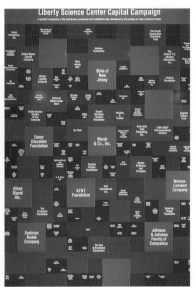

Identity and signage programs, exhibit standards, and marketing communications for Liberty Science Center, Liberty State Park, NJ. The project called for an active, engaging identity that fit the overall educational philosophy of the 150,000-square-foot museum. The team established and coordinated standards throughout the building and exhibits, as well as designed and implemented all building signage, information systems and communications programs. Project team: Nancye Green, Karen Manier, Clint Morgan, Susan Myers, Julie Riefler and Brian Stanlake.

left
Cardmember communications for American Express Travel Related Services Co., Inc., New York, NY. A communication strategy was developed involving consumer publications produced for millions of Cardmembers in six distinctive markets. The "family" of newsletters created provided clear, concise information and graphics targeted to each market.
Project team: Nancye Green, Marge Levin, Susan Myers, Lisa Banks, Paul Carlos, Elizabeth Lyons, Karen Manier, Stacy Margolis, Robert Spica, Brian Stanlake and Lisa Yee.

right
Catalogs for Parsons School of Design, New York, NY. The covers were designed in a way that represented most of Parsons' disciplines. The designer worked as collaborator with the photographers—using typography, images and special lighting projected onto translucent, reflective and opaque surfaces—to create the effect.
Designer: Michael Donovan; photography, Austin Hughes and Amos Chan.

below
City guidebook for Newport, RI. *N: The Newport Guide*, the first in a new series of guidebooks by Richard Saul Wurman, reinvents his earlier guide to landmarks, restaurants, accommodations and local history.
Project team: Richard Saul Wurman, John Grimwade, Vanessa Ryan and Lisa Yee.

left, below left and below
"Information Environment" for 3M, St. Paul, MN. The project provides both a big picture and in-depth presentation of 3M at its corporate headquarters. Key components of the exhibit are interactive programs that trace the evolution of 3M's products and technologies, and explore how 3M's culture actively promotes innovation.
Project team: Michael Donovan, Susan Berman, Jim Kaylor, Adrian Levin, Patrick Nolan, Paul Soulellis and Allen Wilpon.

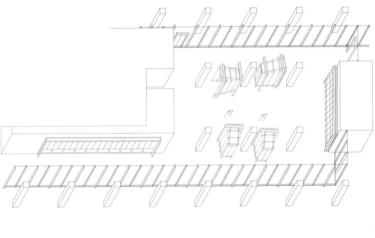

left
Marketing communications, print advertising and traveling exhibition for Wilkhahn Inc., New York/Germany. Wilkhahn, a contract furniture industry leader in Europe for more than 40 years, wanted to introduce and extend its European ideals to the United States marketplace. The entire marketing communications and advertising program was created in nine months, including completely new product photography, copy and design formats.
Project team: Michael Donovan, Austin Hughes, Lynn Saravis, Vanessa Ryan and Allen Wilpon.

Public exhibition for the Ronald Reagan Presidential Library, Simi Valley, CA. Selected by the Ronald Reagan Presidential Foundation, the firm conceived, designed and produced the public exhibition. The 22,000-square-foot exhibition environment is technologically sophisticated, yet intentionally designed not to look high-tech. It is comfortable, friendly and accessible to visitors, permanent staff and docents. Project team: Nancye Green, Michael Donovan, Susan Berman, Susan Myers, Stuart Silver, Steve Brosnahan, Alan Ford, Gabrielle Goodman, Patrick Nolan, Leslie Nowinski, Alexis Siroc, Sheila Szcepaniak and Allen Wilpon.

above and right
Corporate headquarters exhibition for Corning, New York, NY. In developing an entry to Corning's new international corporate headquarters, the firm created a visual experience that metaphorically represented the company. The solution utilizes basic optical principles of science and Corning's state-of-the-art technology—dichroic filters, prisms and optical mirrors combined with computer-controlled point-source lighting.
Project team:
Michael Donovan and Allen Wilpon.

below
NDA Expert System for F. Hoffmann-LaRoche Ltd., Basel, Switzerland. The project consists of six volumes of annotated information on the drug development regulatory process. It comprises the necessary tools, guides and support materials to allow participants to learn from each other's experiences, and to exchange information across scientific disciplines.
Project team: Nancye Green, Marge Levin, Thom Kam, Ray Sysko, Marjorie Nelson; in collaboration with Richard Saul Wurman.

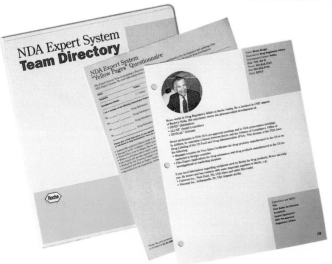

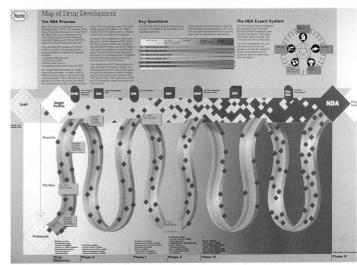

Drenttel Doyle Partners

Principals: Tom Kluepfel,
William Drenttel,
Stephen Doyle
Year Founded: 1985
Size of Firm: 13
Key Clients:
Champion International,
Cooper-Hewitt National
Design Museum,
HarperCollins, Hewitt
Associates, Metropolitan
Transportation Authority,
NYZS/The Wildlife
Conservation Society,
Princeton University,
Saint Vincents Hospital,

Springmaid, The Edison
Project, The World
Financial Center,
Wamsutta.

1123 Broadway
Suite 600
New York, NY 10010
212 463 8787

D renttel Doyle Partners embodies the collision of the worlds of design and marketing. The result is a collaboration focused on creating a dialogue between client and audience, with design solutions rooted in concept, not adornment. This creative tactic often adds layers of meaning, elevating projects from the mundane into the extraordinary—with wit, elegance, and a disciplined approach to problem-solving. Much of the firm's recent work has involved creating dynamic institutional and brand identity programs, public space installations and editorial design for a diverse group of clients.

right
Magazines for Cooper-Hewitt National Design Museum, New York, NY. The magazine's format merged two of the museum's publications—educational programming and the museum's calendar—into one piece.

far right
National Design Museum's "coat check" sign—a second-hand wool overcoat with silk-screened type—combines sign with symbol.

above
Poster announcing a presentation by Drenttel and Doyle for AIGA, Los Angeles, CA. They discussed the nature of their working relationships, as well as the challenges of creating a niche for their firm in the chasm between the worlds of design and business.

left
From left: William Drenttel, Stephen Doyle and Tom Kluepfel. Photography, Ray Charles White.

below left
Was/Saw poster for a lecture at the American Center for Design, Chicago, IL. The rusted saw, with "was" painted in white, references dyslexia, surrealism and the back-and-forth nature of the lecturers' working relationship. It's part of a series of personal explorations into the relationships between word and object, sign and symbol.

below right
Poster to promote colors of "Benefit" paper for Champion International, Stamford, CT.

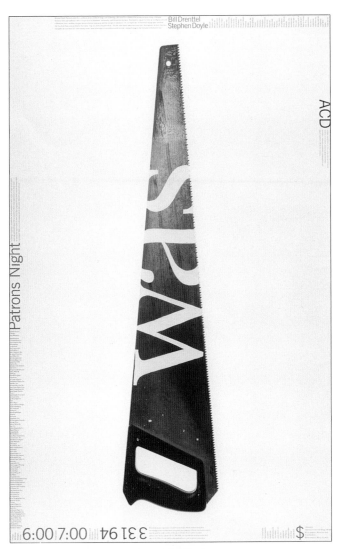

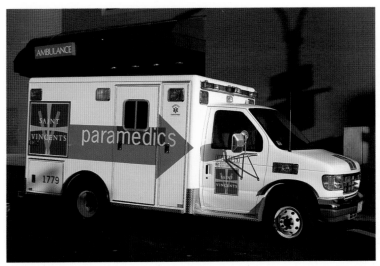

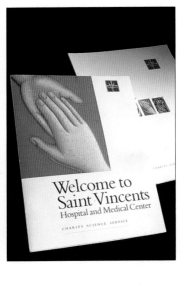

left
Identity program for Saint Vincents Hospital, New York, NY. The identity helps to reflect the dynamic work and the heritage of the 150-year-old institution.

above
Installation celebrating the
75th Anniversary of
women's suffrage for the
New York State Division
for Women. The installation
applied actual text from the
19th Amendment in 8-foot
letters to the marble floor
of Grand Central Terminal.
A 20-foot propaganda tower
displayed epherma, large-
scale images of suffragists
and historical text.

below
New York Transit Museum
Gift Shop and Information
Center, main concourse,
Grand Central Terminal,
for the Metropolitan Transporation Authority. Seen
by thousands of commuters
daily, the transportable shop
encourages people to look
at MTA in a new way. The
design and materials work
together to create a machine-
like effect, suggestive of
high-speed trains and urban
transportation. The effect is
reinforced by illustrator

Brian Cronin's vibrant
urban mural. It acts like
a visual magnet from across
the concourse. The shop,
fabricated by MTA crafts-
people, is made entirely from
surplus supplies from MTA
stockyards.

above
Books for The Edison
Project, New York, NY, a
privately-sponsored initia-
tive for managing public
schools in partnership with
local communities. The
design program is meant to
reflect the accessible, inquis-
itive and forward-thinking
nature of an Edison educa-
tion. The design contains
the ability to gracefully
expand over time by using
variable colors and changing
color bands.

left
Wamsutta Elite sheet packaging for Spring Industries,
New York, NY. As part of
a large "branding" design
review, the Elite line was
designed to reflect a high-
end product.

above
Packaging of gourmet
foods for Agata and
Valentina, New York, NY.
The packaging program
included pasta, jams, juices
and bakery items.

bottom left
ABC, for Hyperion Books
for Children, New York,
NY. The exceptional collection of photographs exem-
plifies Wegman's style—
a combination of humor,
elegance and originality.

bottom right
Poster advertising a theater
production for Creative
Productions, New York, NY.

right
Annual report for NYZS/
The Wildlife Conservation
Society, Bronx, NY.

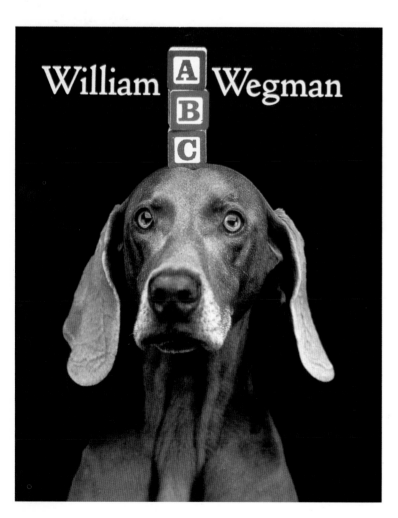

right and above
Architectural installation, part of the World Financial Center's "Celebrate Prague" Festival, for Olympia & York, New York, NY. The detached blue entrance structure is distorted to create a tunnel-like passageway into a visual reflection of a city; the design of a "room within a room" conveys the sense of being on the inside looking out, as well as being on the outside looking in.

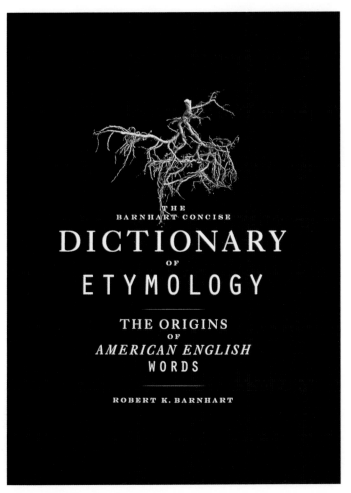

left
This dictionary, for Harper-Collins, New York, NY, traces the "roots" of words.

right
This flyer—distributed in 4,000 bookstores across the U.S.—brings attention to the fifth anniversary of the Iranian decree that called for the death of British writer Salman Rushdie.

Eric Baker Design Associates

Principals: Eric Baker
Year Founded: 1986
Size of Firm: 7
Key Clients: Alfred A. Knopf,
Blue Note Records, Bulfinch
Press, Chronicle Books,
Delphi Internet, Doubleday,
Gilbert Paper, MTV
Networks, Naked Angels
Theatre Group, Random
House, Saturday Night Live,
Simon & Schuster.

11 East 22nd Street
New York, NY 10010
212 598 9111

Eric Baker Design Associates' spirit lies in a deeply-rooted love for books and an uncompromising desire to create them, but the firm's strength and interests also trend towards projects such as exhibit catalogs, web site design, multimedia, paper promotions, identity programs and packaging design. The cultural diversity and talent of the staff contributes to the fresh approach brought to each project led by principal Eric Baker, who is an active member and award winner in the graphic design community. Baker's work has appeared in a plethora of art and design publications, he has co-authored several books and is a two-time recipient of the National Endowment for the Arts Design grant for his independent design-history projects. Believing that the inspiration of design comes from within the project rather than an applied aesthetic, the result is a wide range of work in publishing and corporate communications—constantly evolving to suit the rapidly changing role graphic design presents in society.

above
Cover and book design for Joyce Tenneson's photographs, Bulfinch Press, Boston, MA. The book is an exhibition of the photographer's personal work. All the original images are Polaroid, 20-by-30 inches. Designer, Eric Baker.

left
From left—front row:
Ingrid Forbord, Eric Baker,
Principal; and Rymn
Massand. Back row: Robert
Hudson, Jason Godfrey and
Greg Simpson.
Photography,
Ray Charles White.

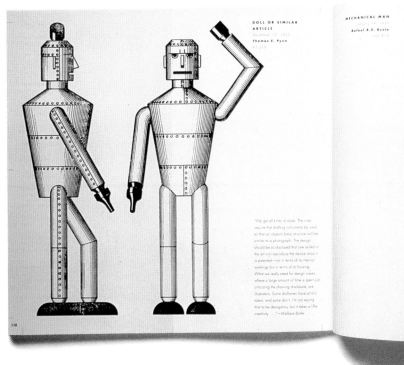

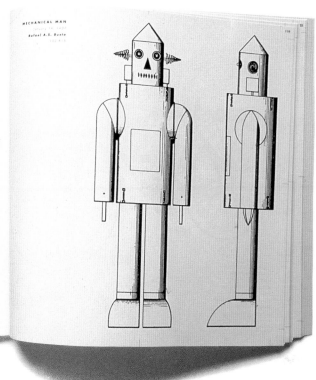

left and bottom left
Cover and spread design in
the book *Great Inventions-
Good Intentions*, Chronicle
Books, San Francisco, CA.
The book shows an over-
view of "design patents"
(patents granted for the design of an object rather than
its mechanical function)
produced from 1930-1949.
Designers, Eric Baker
and Chip Kidd.

left
Cover of the Herb Ritts
Calendar, Bulfinch Press,
Boston, MA.
Designers, Eric Baker
and Patrick Seymour.

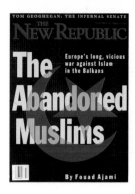

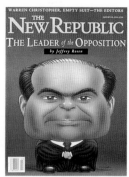

left and below
Magazine covers for
The New Republic,
Washington D.C. The
weekly news magazine
focuses on current events
and political issues.
Design Director,
Eric Baker.

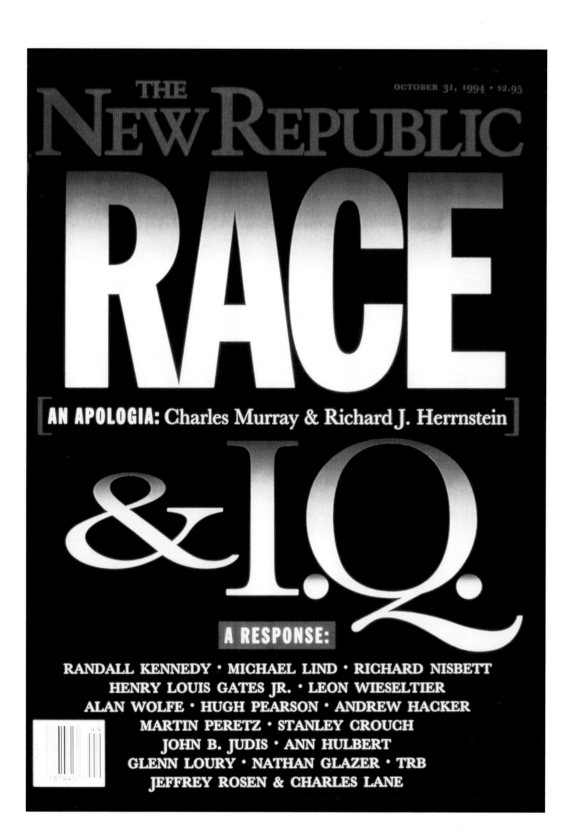

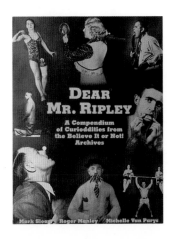

Cover and book design for *Dear Mr. Ripley*, Bulfinch Press, Boston, MA. Designers, Eric Baker and Kai Zimmerman.

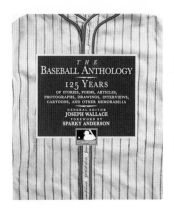

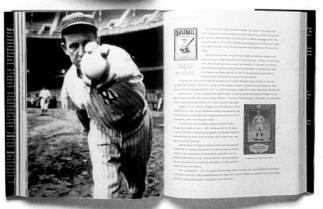

Cover and book design for *The Baseball Anthology*, Harry N. Abrams, New York, NY. Designers, Eric Baker and Patrick Seymour.

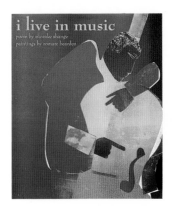

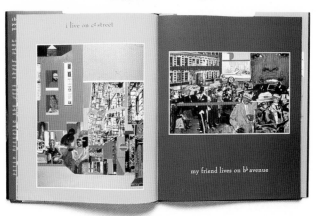

Cover and book design for *I Live in Music*, Stuart, Tabori and Chang, New York, NY. Designers, Eric Baker; paintings by, Romare Bearden; poetry, Ntozake Shange.

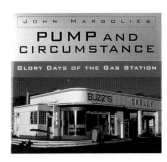

Cover and book design for *Pump and Circumstance*, Bullfinch Press. Designers, Eric Baker and Kai Zimmerman.

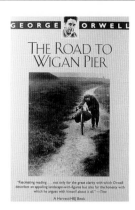

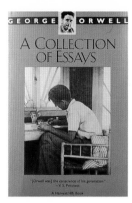

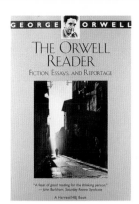

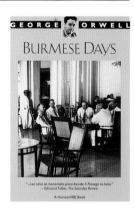

right
Book jackets created for a
series style of George Orwell
books, Harcourt Brace
Jovanovich, New York, NY.
Designer, Eric Baker;
vintage photos, Bill Brant,
Henri Cartier Breson,
Magnum, and
Bruce Richardson.

below
Book jacket designs for
The End of Laissez-Faire
and *Freud's Vienna & Other
Essays*, Alfred A. Knopf,
New York, NY.
Designer, Eric Baker.

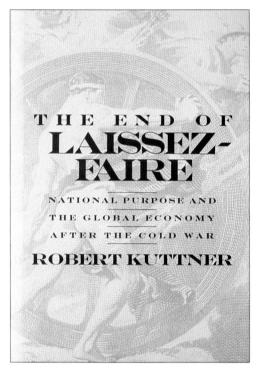

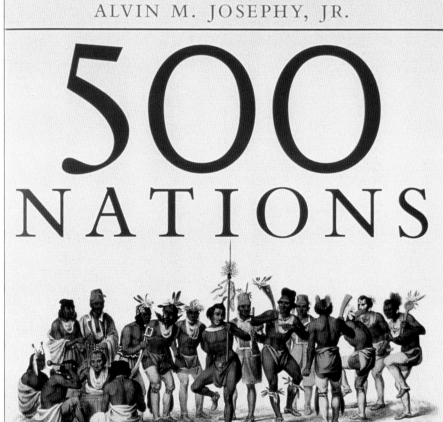

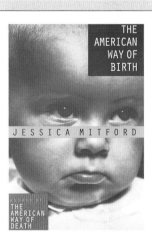

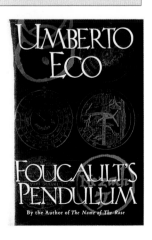

bottom/opposite page
Book jacket designs for *500 Nations*, Alfred A. Knopf, New York, NY. Designers, Eric Baker and Kai Zimmerman.

George Bush's War, Henry Holt, New York, NY. Designer, Eric Baker.

The American Way of Birth, Penguin Books, New York, NY. Designer, Eric Baker.

Foucaults Pendulum, Harcourt, Brace, Jovanovich, San Diego, CA. Designer, Eric Baker.

PANTONE

far left
Logo for Pantone, Inc. New Jersey. Designer, Eric Baker; illustrator, Jean Tuttle.

left
Promotional logo for Alfred A. Knopf, New York, NY. Designer, Eric Baker.

below
Logo for the music studio, Flying Monkey, New York, NY. Designer, Eric Baker.

Greetings From New York

above/far left
Logo for a photography gallery, Houk Friedman Galleries, New York, NY. Designer, Eric Baker.

far left
T-shirt design for and by Eric Baker, New York, NY.

left
Logo for Bennetton's 25th-Anniversary, New York, NY. Designer, Eric Baker, illustrator, David Diaz.

SUMMARY OF ACCOUNT

Amount due on previo...

Payment as of

Previously due

CURRENT BILLIN

Electric charg

NVOICES PAST 30 DAYS WIL
CE CHARGE OF 1 1/2% PER
NUAL PERCENTAGE OF 18%.

TOTAL DUE

Y MI 48007-7011

IS AMOUNT DUE UPON RECEIPT

13.00 PAY THIS AMOUNT

OUR ACCOUNT IS
KINDLY DISREGAR
THE TIMES SERVE
SAVINGS AT OVER
1-800-NYTIMES FOR DETAILS ABOUT

; WILL BE SUBJECT TO A
PER MONTH WHICH IS
8%.

ORIGINIAL INVOICE

$313.08

DUE THIS MONTH		31-60 DAYS
		42.96
CURRENT		169.30
TOTAL AMOUNT		212.26
212.26		

56.18

13.0

ALL IN
FINANCE
AN ANNU
NVOICE

T DUE--P
OTICE IF
5% RESTA
STAURANT

No Radio

Frankfurt Balkind

Partners:
Steve Frankfurt, Chairman;
Aubrey Balkind, CEO;
Philip Dubrow, Vice
Chairman; Peter Bemis,
President (LA);
Smitty, President (LA);
Kent Hunter, Executive
Creative Director;
Andreas Combüchen,
Creative Director;
Harriet Levin, Executive
Vice President
Founded: 1972
Size of Firm: 130

Clients:
ABC, Avon, EG&G,
Gartner Group, The Getty,
LG (Korea), Novell, Saks
Fifth Ave, Seagate, Sony,
Towers Perrin, NCR.

244 East 58th Street
New York, NY 10022
212 421 5888
www.frankfurtbalkind.com

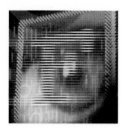

rankfurt Balkind Partners is a strategic communications agency focused on the convergence of information, entertainment and technology and its impact upon corporate and mass culture. The agency is comprised of communications experts at the top of their fields. They've come together for the express purpose of developing and executing innovative answers to marketing problems in a changing world. With offices located in America's major centers of influence—New York City (financial, marketing, publishing, the arts); Los Angeles (entertainment); and San Francisco (Silicon Valley)—Frankfurt Balkind keeps on top of the trends and ideas that influence culture worldwide today.

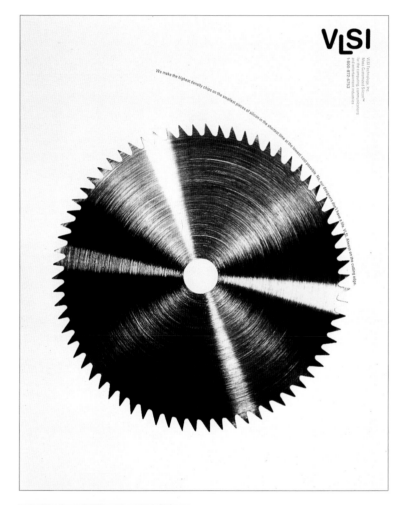

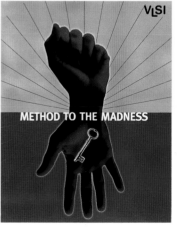

METHOD TO THE MADNESS

above and left
Positioning, identity and advertising for VLSI Technology, Inc., San Jose, CA. To position VLSI on the "cutting edge" of the industry segment, "mass-customized silicon" was expressed through advertising that ran in business and trade publications, a capabilities brochure, and an annual report.

above
From left:
Steve Frankfurt, Kent Hunter,
Tracey Woodcock, Kin Yuen,
Philip Durbrow,
Andreas Combüchen, and
Aubrey Balkind.
Photography,
Ray Charles White.

right
Redesign and relaunch of
the @vantage Web site for
Gartner Group, Stamford,
CT, an independent
information technology
consultancy. @vantage subscribers use the site to access
research and analysis from
Gartner and other leading
technology consultants.
Agency work for Gartner
also includes a CD-ROM
product and videos for the
annual Gartner symposium.

left and right
Video and annual report for
Seagate Technology, Inc.,
Scotts Valley, CA, the
world's leading manufacturer
of hard drives. Designed to
help raise Seagate's (and the
storage industry's) low P/E
ratio, the annual report and
video highlight the barriers
to entry in the storage
industry, explain why disk
drives are not a commodity
and show how the need for
storage will increase dramatically as computers are asked
to "communicate more like
you and me."

below right
Corporate repositioning
and identity for Novell, Inc.,
Orem, UT. New positioning,
extended graphically to the
new identity, communicates
that this global networking
leader "connects people
with the people and information they need." It is the
platform for an integrated
communications campaign
designed to build recognition
of the Novell brand in
emerging and business-to-
business markets.

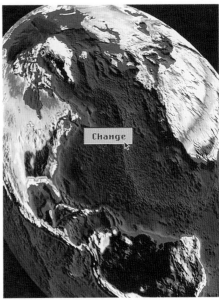

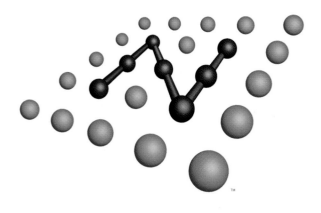

Novell

left and below
Annual reports and meetings for The Limited, Columbus, OH. The Limited's annual meetings, attended by more than 8,000 employees and a host of securities analysts, are used to reinforce its unique corporate culture. Themes introduced in the annual report are extended to the meeting through integrated videos, promotions, music and collateral materials.

left
Corporate identity and advertising, product identity, packaging and advertising, direct marketing and point-of-purchase materials for Pantone, Inc., the leading developer of color specification standards for the creative industry. Shown are ads from two campaigns: "Sunflower" is part of an image campaign designed to raise awareness of the Pantone brand; "Bubblegum" is one in a series of ads targeted at textile designers.

above
Screens from an interactive touch-screen kiosk showcasing products for Sharp Electronics. First installed at Sharp's corporate headquarters to help launch a new 14-inch flat-screen technology, it is now used at trade shows and conventions across the country.

left
World*business*, a custom publication for KMPG Peat Marwick, New York, NY. Positioned, named and designed to strengthen the company's reputation as a leader in global business consulting, this journalistically independent magazine presents coverage of international business issues targeted at senior managers. Although not originally conceived as a profit center, it has recently begun accepting advertising in exclusive categories.

right
Web site for Cowen & Company, New York, NY, a financial services company focused on the technology, health care, entertainment and media industries. The "dynamic" site (built in real time using 15-minute delayed stock data) features the Cowen Internet Index, and other tools clients can use to manage their portfolios.

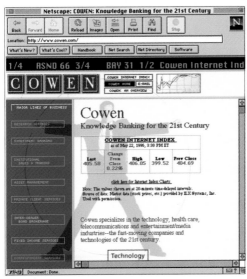

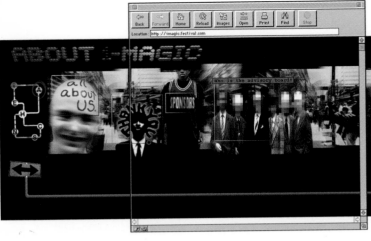

Seriousness is the only refuge of the shallow.

Motion pictures reach one of the largest mass markets of any new "product." Frankfurt Balkind creates over 25 motion picture advertising campaigns each year for the major studios.

THE ANIMAL IS OUT

NICHOLSON
PFEIFFER

a Mike Nichols film

WOLF

COMING SOON

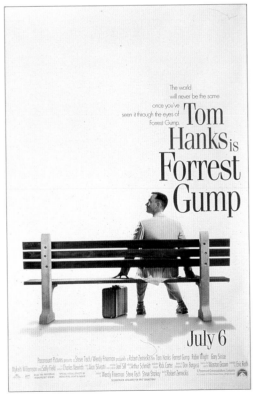

The world will never be the same once you've seen it through the eyes of Forrest Gump.

Tom
HANKS is
Forrest
Gump

July 6

left and opposite page
Web site for i-Magic, New York, NY, the interactive industry's first major awards festival. Created to promote the festival, provide program information and facilitate communication among members of the interactive community, the site features a "New York" look and feel and entertaining interactivity (such as the fortune cookie, opposite page, that produces a fortune to "reward" exploration of the "About i-Magic" screen).

right
Direct mail catalog strategy, positioning and design for Avon Products Inc., New York, NY. A new sales channel for Avon, this catalog updates the company's image, appealing to the younger, more sophisticated consumer. It is distributed to over one million women each quarter.

left
Capabilities brochure for LG (formerly Lucky Goldstar), Korea's third-largest conglomerate. The brochure describes LG's rapid expansion into the international marketplace and outlines the factors that will push its revenues from the current $64 billion to a projected $385 billion by the year 2005.

below
Identity, design and development of the online shopping mall DreamShop, for Time Warner, New York, NY. Screens guide you to the online "catalogs" of premium merchants such as Spiegel, Eddie Bauer, Horchow; "Personal Shopper" tools allow you to quickly search the mall for desired items.

LG before 1996

LG in 1996 and after

Jessica Helfand Studio, Ltd.

Principal: Jessica Helfand
Year Founded: 1994
Size of Firm: 3
Key Clients: The New York Times, The Discovery Channel, Champion International Corporation, The Smithsonian Museum of The American Indian, HarperCollins, Knight Ridder Newspapers.

214 Sullivan Street
Suite 6C
New York, NY 10012
212 388 1863
www.jhstudio.com

essica Helfand Studio is a small design consultancy that concentrates on editorial design and the development of new models for new media. In an effort to better define and articulate the impact of technology on design professions, Jessica Helfand is a contributing editor to both *Eye* and *ID* magazines, and has been a visiting lecturer in interaction design at The Cooper Union and New York University's Program in Interactive Telecommunications. Her focus and studio lies in mapping a new kind of editorial process for the strategic development of electronic media, including CD-ROMs, internet web sites, and theoretical projects that introduce alternative conceptual paradigms for communication design.

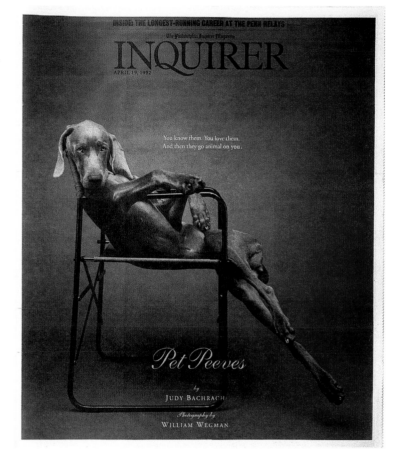

above
Cover for *The Philadelphia Inquirer Magazine*, Philadelphia, PA.
Art Director, Jessica Helfand; writer, Judy Bachrach; photography, William Wegman.

left
Experimental book project on TS Eliot for The Beinecke Rare Book Library, New Haven, CT. The goal was to find a new way to visualize biography by challenging its classical chronological structure.
Art Director, Jessica Helfand.

left
Jessica Helfand in her studio.
Photography,
Ray Charles White.

below
Poster for AIGA/
Philadelphia, PA.
Art Director, Jessica Helfand;
illustrator, Eric Dinyer.

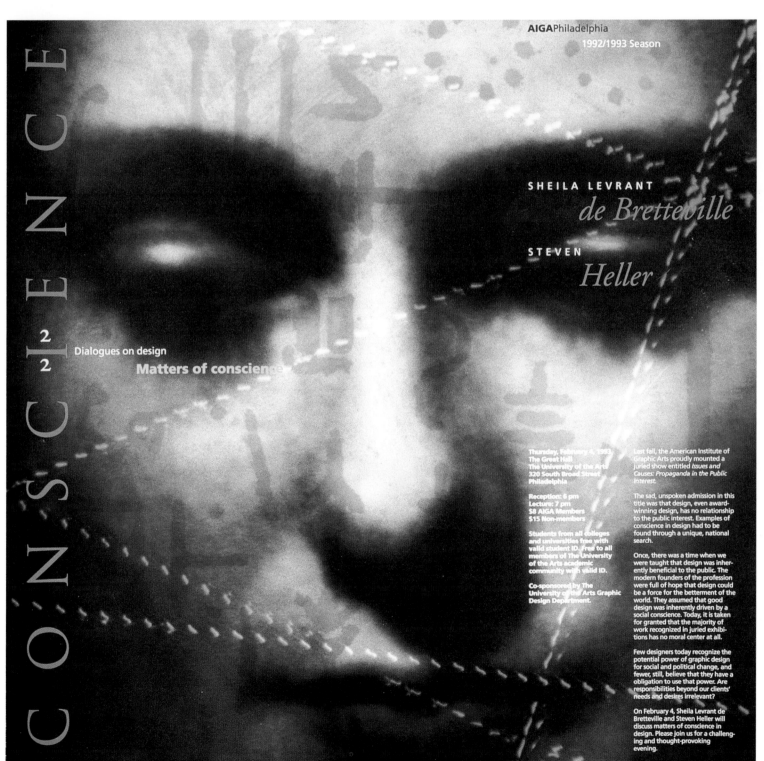

AIGAPhiladelphia
1992/1993 Season

SHEILA LEVRANT
de Bretteville

STEVEN
Heller

CONSCIENCE

2
2

Dialogues on design
Matters of conscience

Thursday, February 4, 1993
The Great Hall
The University of the Arts
320 South Broad Street
Philadelphia

Reception: 6 pm
Lecture: 7 pm
$8 AIGA Members
$15 Non-members

Students from all colleges
and universities free with
valid student ID. Free to all
members of The University
of the Arts academic
community with valid ID.

Co-sponsored by The
University of the Arts Graphic
Design Department.

Last fall, the American Institute of
Graphic Arts proudly mounted a
juried show entitled *Issues and
Causes: Propaganda in the Public
Interest.*

The sad, unspoken admission in this
title was that design, even award-
winning design, has no relationship
to the public interest. Examples of
conscience in design had to be
found through a unique, national
search.

Once, there was a time when we
were taught that design was inherently beneficial to the public. The
modern founders of the profession
were full of hope that design could
be a force for the betterment of the
world. They assumed that good
design was inherently driven by a
social conscience. Today, it is taken
for granted that the majority of
work recognized in juried exhibitions has no moral center at all.

Few designers today recognize the
potential power of graphic design
for social and political change, and
fewer, still, believe that they have a
obligation to use that power. Are
responsibilities beyond our clients'
needs and desires irrelevant?

On February 4, Sheila Levrant de
Bretteville and Steven Heller will
discuss matters of conscience in
design. Please join us for a challenging and thought-provoking
evening.

below

Representative screens from *Talking Pictures*, Lookout, New York, NY. As a companion to an exhibition that toured twelve U.S. cities, and a catalog published by Chronicle Books, an interactive teaching guide was created that focused on the idea that still pictures have the capacity to be more emotionally moving than moving pictures. Art Director, Jessica Helfand; producers, Carole Kismaric and Marvin Heiferman.

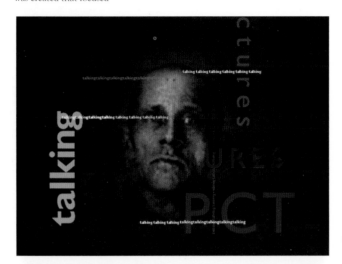

Born in 1857, Eugene Atget is best known for capturing the spirit of Paris in his photographs. In all, he took over ten thousand pictures over nearly forty years. His prey was more elusive you might expect: Atget photographed the old city, its brothels and doorways and dirty fountains, the stages on which its daily drama was played out. Atget stopped to absorb the detail that others failed to notice, but he couldn't have cared less about seeing the sights. Not once in forty years did he photograph the Eiffel Tower. There is no mistaking an Atget photograph, but no easy means of describing it either; he seems to impose no style, and yet no one else, faced with the same scene, could ever have arrived at the same likeness.

He is known, sometimes dismissively, for his conjuring of atmosphere; The edges of his buildings are pure and hard, unbothered by background fuss but as you look into the distance the light relaxes into a feathery haze. You are left with the extraordinary sensation that perspective is a matter not only of space but of real time as well; perhaps in front of your eyes it is high noon, but day seems to be breaking at the end every street. Proust or Eliot? Surrealism or fetishization? Atget the businessman or Atget the bum? Every cast of thought, every emotional strategy, it seems, has remade him in its own image. In the end, Atget's Paris lies somewhere between Baudelaire and the Baedeker, a guided tour to one man's imagination.

◄ Go back   Visit Atget's Paris ►

SEPT 30, 1995
MONDAY

Job Market

CLICK ON ANY
ARTICLE

The New York Times

CAREERS

HELP WANTED

New This Week

Career&
Family:
Keeping
Balance

Getting Wired
for the
Revolution

The I.B.M.
Circle: Unbroken

Stalking a Useful
Career Guide

Click to Search Classifieds

| Home | Quick Read | Late News | About NYT | Feedback | Help |

The New York Times
Arts *&* Entertainment Guide

Film   Music & Dance   Theater

Books of   Dining   Museums
The Times   Out   & Galleries

Search   Message
Boards

@times main screen

left
Screens from *The New York Times* sites on The World Wide Web and America OnLine. The goal was to create an identity that recalled the elegance and efficiency of the paper's typography and limited color palette.
Art Director, Jessica Helfand; editors, Kevin McKenna and Elliott Rebhun.

Home Page for *Shift OnLine* (since retitled word.com), New York, NY, a "digizine" on the World Wide Web. Black and white photographic icons were created in the form of a travelling bookmark: content in the wide column "shifts" from place to place, while the left-hand panel remains visible throughout the reader's journey.
Art Director, Jessica Helfand; producer, Dan Pelson; editor, Jonathan Van Meter.

atm

monitor

brain

map

etcetera

work

planet

labs

domain

voyeur

shift online

menu

Crack

and the **Investment Banker**

| The ABC Generation | Head Games |

To Protect & Serve
A day with a 27-year-old
cop in Los Angeles

**The Death of
Saturday Night Live**
Has twenty years of sketches
come to this?

SATURDAY · NIGHT · LIVE

Where I'm From
Monster Kody Scott writes
from solitary confinement

full spread
Representative screens from Discovery Channel Online, Bethesda, MD, a comprehensive editorial site for Discovery Communications on The World Wide Web. Here, a story on Eadweard Muybridge used the photographer's sequenced images as simple flip-book animations.

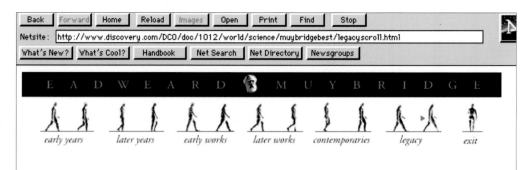

Back | Forward | Home | Reload | Images | Open | Print | Find | Stop

Netsite: http://www.discovery.com/DCO/doc/1012/world/science/muybridgebest/legacyscroll.html

What's New? | What's Cool? | Handbook | Net Search | Net Directory | Newsgroups

E A D W E A R D   M U Y B R I D G E

early years | *later years* | *early works* | *later works* | *contemporaries* | *legacy* | *exit*

Legacy

Muybridge's Legacy

Eadweard Muybridge was not a scientist: He merely masqueraded as one. The motion studies were not conducted under laboratory conditions, and Eadweard had no qualms about fudging data; he duplicated, replaced, or renumbered frames in more than a third of his studies. Some sequences were not captured but posed.

...elations, what are we to make of Muybridge?

...Muybridge was the first to develop a system for taking a series ...f objects in rapid motion. He also was the first to reproduce and ...n by projecting sequential photos on a screen.

...y, Muybridge was one of the first to explore the no-man's-land ...and art. All his inventions were means to artistic ends, and ...influence has been most keenly felt. Motion pictures, medical ...d comic book art developed from conventions Muybridge

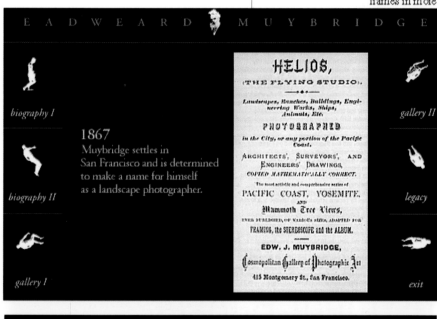

E A D W E A R D   M U Y B R I D G E

biography I

biography II

gallery I

1867
Muybridge settles in San Francisco and is determined to make a name for himself as a landscape photographer.

HELIOS,
(THE FLYING STUDIO).

Landscapes, Ranches, Buildings, Engineering Works, Ships, Animals, Etc.

PHOTOGRAPHED

in the City, or any portion of the Pacific Coast.

ARCHITECTS', SURVEYORS', AND ENGINEERS' DRAWINGS,
COPIED MATHEMATICALLY CORRECT.

The most artistic and comprehensive series of

PACIFIC COAST, YOSEMITE,
AND
Mammoth Tree Views,

EVER PUBLISHED, OF VARIOUS SIZES, ADAPTED FOR FRAMING, the STEREOSCOPE and the ALBUM.

EDW. J. MUYBRIDGE,

Cosmopolitan Gallery of Photographic Art

415 Montgomery St., San Francisco.

gallery II

legacy

exit

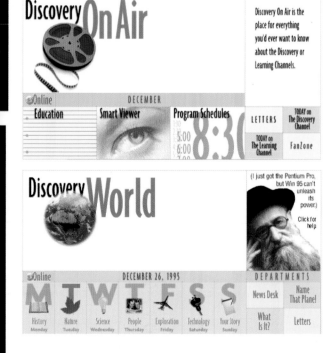

Discovery On Air

Discovery On Air is the place for everything you'd ever want to know about the Discovery or Learning Channels.

Online
Education | DECEMBER | Smart Viewer | Program Schedules
5:00
6:00 | 8:30

LETTERS | TODAY on The Discovery Channel
TODAY on The Learning Channel | FanZone

Discovery World

(I just got the Pentium Pro, but Win 95 can't unleash its power.)
Click for help

Online | DECEMBER 26, 1995 | DEPARTMENTS
M T W T F S S
History Monday | Nature Tuesday | Science Wednesday | People Thursday | Exploration Friday | Technology Saturday | Your Story Sunday

News Desk | Name That Plane!
What Is It? | Letters

E a d w e a r d   M u y b r i d g e

animated intro

story overview

Representative screens from Discovery Channel Online. Creative Director, Jessica Helfand; art director, Melissa Tardiff; producer, Lucy Kneebone; technical director, Amnon Dekel; designers: Irwin Chen, Saba Ghazi-Ameen, Anne Kim, Christian Luis, Loreena Persaud and Kathryn Poteet; programmers: Tirtza Even, Sue Johnson, Yair Sageev, Miriam Songster and Christopher Vail

A History of the Internet
How Did We Get Here Anyway?

From ARPANET to archie, from nuclear war to netscape: the whole anarchic mess in one neat little timeline.

By Daniel P. Dern
Illustrations by James Kraus
continue

We're Going Down!

Just a hundred feet into the air, the controls stopped responding. There was only the Burmese jungle between us and disaster.

By Stanley Gates

continue

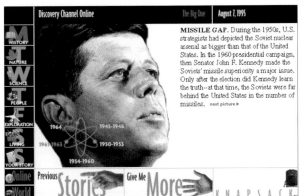

Discovery Channel Online   The Big One   August 7, 1995

MISSILE GAP. During the 1950s, U.S. strategists had depicted the Soviet nuclear arsenal as bigger than that of the United States. In the 1960 presidential campaign, then Senator John F. Kennedy made the Soviets' missile superiority a major issue. Only after the election did Kennedy learn the truth--at that time, the Soviets were far behind the United States in the number of missiles. next picture ▶

1964   1945-1948
1961-1963   1950-1953
1954-1960

Online   Previous Stories   Give Me More   KNAPSACK
World

Discovery Channel Online   The Big One   August 7, 1995

NIKITA KHRUSHCHEV. During a 1956 speech to Western diplomats in Moscow, the Soviet premier spoke the phrase that heightened fears about Soviet aggression: "We base ourselves on the idea that we must peacefully co-exist. About the capitalist states, it doesn't depend on you whether or not we exist...whether you like it or not, history is on our side. We will bury you." next picture ▶

1964   1945-1948
1961-1963   1950-1953
1954-1960

Online   Previous Stories   Give Me More   KNAPSACK
World

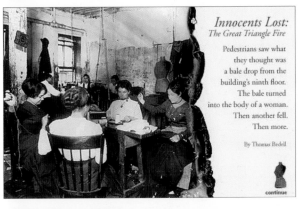

Innocents Lost:
The Great Triangle Fire

Pedestrians saw what they thought was a bale drop from the building's ninth floor. The bale turned into the body of a woman. Then another fell. Then more.

By Thomas Bedell

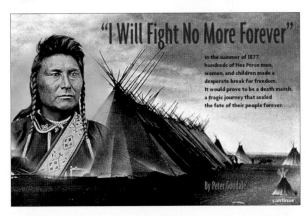

"I Will Fight No More Forever"

In the summer of 1877, hundreds of Nez Perce men, women, and children made a desperate break for freedom. It would prove to be a death march, a tragic journey that sealed the fate of their people forever.

By Peter Goodale

continue

SUMMER THUNDER
Story by
JANE WATERHOUSE

Continue

Landor Associates

Principals: Allen Adamson, Richard Brandt, Pamela Abitbol, Victoria Arzano, Hayes Roth, Alice Coxe, Laura Bobbitt
Year Founded: 1941
New York office: 1978
Size of Firm: 350
New York office: 47
Key Clients: AT&T, Eastman Kodak, FedEx, L'Oréal, Nestlé/Stouffer's, PepsiCo, Pfizer, Philip Morris, Procter & Gamble, Sara Lee, Titleist and Foot-Joy, Xerox.

230 Park Avenue South
Seventh Floor
New York, NY 10003
212 614 5050
www.landor.com

Landor Associates, an internationally recognized design leader, has full service design offices in New York, San Francisco, Seattle, London, Paris, Hong Kong, Tokyo and Mexico City. Landor works for hundreds of clients across dozens of industries on nearly every continent. The firm believes design is one of the most efficient and effective forms of communication. A single image, powerfully rendered, can burn itself into the collective conscious and remain there for a lifetime, influencing behavior and decisions through the emotions it summons. Landor harnesses design's immense power to capture and communicate a brand's core essence. With design that is intelligently crafted and strategically executed, it hopes to provoke visceral responses that compel people to act. "Products are made in the factory, but brands are created in the mind," said Walter Landor, who founded the firm in 1941. To this day, Landor Associates still creates, builds and renews some of the world's most recognized and respected brands.

left
Worldwide identity renewal for Federal Express Corp., Memphis, TN. The corporation needed to better communicate its global capabilities, varied service offerings, and stature as the industry's founder and leader. The design leverages one of the company's greatest assets—the "FedEx" brand name. Landor had the company adopt FedEx as its official communicative name to appear across all applications and media. For a company that operates in 187 countries, Landor created "The World On Time" tagline as part of the program to reinforce FedEx's worldwide scope.

left
front row: Pamela Abitbol
and Gail Henning;
back row: Allen Adamson,
Laura Bobbitt, Richard
Brandt, Victoria Arzano
and Alice Coxe.

The new FedEx identity is
bolder than the previously
stacked, diagonal logo. It
gives more consistency and
impact when applied on
vehicles, aircraft, packaging,
signage, and in mail-order
catalogs. The FedEx word-
mark is a specially-designed
typeface based on Futura
and Univers. The distinctive
purple and orange colors
were kept, but enhanced for
more impact. Embedded in
the wordmark is an arrow
to convey a sense of speed
and urgency.
Executive Creative
Director, Courtney Reeser;
senior design director,
Lindon Leader; designers,
Jennifer Bostic and Wally
Krantz; environmental
design director, Scott
Drummond; implementa-
tion director, Bruce
McGovert; senior consultant,
Charles Rashall.

International brand revitalization for Pepsi-Cola, Somers, NY. The new blue design (implemented outside of North America) incorporates a modified Pepsi logotype and a distinctive grid pattern to give it a futuristic look. The globe graphic—a reinterpretation of the familiar Pepsi ball—embodies Pepsi's position as a leading global brand, now marketing itself as a choice for "future generations" as well as the present. Creative Director, Richard Brandt; senior designer, Victor Hunt; account manager, Ashley Roberts.

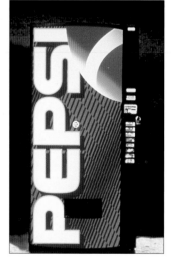

Brand identity for Smooth Moos Smoothies, Pepsi-Cola Company, Somers, NY. Sporting red high-top sneakers and a cool, slightly mischievous grin, young kids enjoy Spot's cartoon charisma while his personality appeals to image-conscious teens.
Creative Director, Richard Brandt; senior designer, Carl Mazer; senior consultant, Pamela Abitbol; illustrator, Joakim Hannerz; photography, Robb Debenport.

left and below
Brand name, positioning and identity for Devil Mountain Brewing Co. Landor worked with Devil Mountain Brewing Co. to develop the optimal positioning, name and packaging for a dynamic and intriguing new microbrew, appropriately named Devil Mountain Ale.
Creative Director, Richard Brandt; senior designer, Jeremy Dawkins; account manager, Amy Barnum; photography, Carolyn Vaughn.

left
Package design targeted to brides and bridal party members for Hanes Hosiery, Winston-Salem, NC. A traditional stocking box becomes a beautiful keepsake. Hot-stamped gold creates a ribbon effect around a gold-toned, rose-patterned box. The bridal party's hosiery packaging adapts the graphic design to a traditional hosiery envelope, reinforcing the product's image.
Creative Director, Richard Brandt; senior design director, Victoria Arzano; senior designer, Chung Lui; senior consultant, Pamela Abitbol.

below
Corporate identity for Sonrisa Skin, Hair and Body Care, and brand development for its product lines: Tropicana, Herbotanics and Aromaflora, Merlite Industries, New York, NY. Sonrisa's logotype and woodcut sun symbol support the premium, organic positioning of its natural beauty care products. The individual graphic identity of each product line evokes the imagery of its particular ingredients.
Executive Creative Director, Kip Reynolds; design directors, Joanna Feldheim and Victoria Arzano; photography, Robb Debenport.

opposite page right
Worldwide corporate identity for Xerox, Stamford, CT. The partially-digitized red X provides Xerox with a compelling symbol that represents its commitment to technology and visually articulates the diversity of its products and services. Executive Creative Director, Courtney Reeser; creative director, Margaret Youngblood; senior design director and designer, Margo Zucker; designer, Nancy Zeches.

below
Corporate identity for A Better Chance, New York, NY. The organization provides educational opportunities to promising minority children. A simple, child-like drawing captures the dreams and wonder that children feel when gazing at the stars, and reflects the hope the organization offers. Creative Director, Richard Brandt; senior designer, Carl Mazer.

bottom left
Brand identity for L'Oréal Professional Salon Products, New York, NY. Targeted to professional stylists and sold in beauty supply stores, the Nature's Therapy identity introduces spa-like imagery into a category dominated by commodity packaging, while conveying the product's botanical qualities. Creative Director, Richard Brandt; senior design director, Victoria Arzano; senior designer, Lori Yi; consultant, Ashley Roberts.

bottom right
Brand identity for Sutter Home Winery, St. Helena, CA. The redesign introduces a clear label against a flint glass bottle, showcasing the wine's color and providing a cleaner presentation of Sutter Home's familiar logo. A new finish for the bottle's neck eliminates lead foil wrapping. Instead, a protective clear wrap is used to display the cork. Executive Creative Director, Courtney Reeser; senior designer, Peter Matsukawa; illustrator, Ed Boll; photography, Robb Debenport.

Louise Fili Ltd.

Principal: Louise Fili
Year Founded: 1989
Size of Firm: 4
Key clients: Arista Records,
Ark Restaurants, Bartlett
Winery, L. Bogdanow
Associates, Chronicle Books,
El Paso Chile Co.,
Estee Lauder, Espace,
Prix Fixe, Picholine,
Sony Music, Zelda.

71 Fifth Avenue
New York, NY 10003
212 989 9153

Louise Fili—a typographer and designer of posters, books and book jackets for the past five years—has focused her talents on the design of food packages, wine labels and restaurant identities. Here is a collection of Fili's most recent works; each not merely an aesthetic "tour de force," but an intelligently composed graphic personality—custom solutions that begin with her unique approach to type and image. As a co-author of books on Italian, French and American Art Deco graphic design, Fili draws upon historical influences and rare typefaces which are both transformed into contemporary designs and that insure immediate and memorable responses.

above
"Louise Fili Cincinnati"
poster design for the
Cincinnati Art Directors
Club, OH.
Designer, Louise Fili;
photography, Ed Spiro.

below
Modernism & Eclecticism,
a poster for a design history
symposium at the School of
Visual Arts, New York, NY.
Designer, Louise Fili.

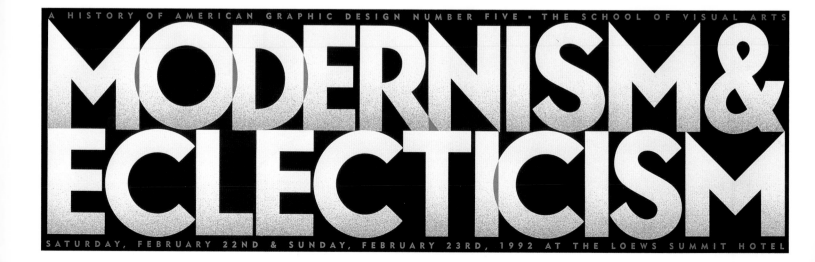

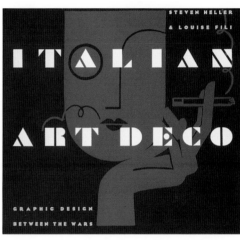

above
Dutch Moderne, Streamline and *Italian Art Deco*; three in a series of books on historical graphic design styles, co-authored with Steven Heller and designed by

Louise Fili. Published by Chronicle Books, San Francisco, CA.

below
A promotional booklet for Richard Solomon, New York, NY, an illustrator's representative. The logo was "re-emphasized" by foil-stamping it on black

board with die-cut eyes to reveal the "O's" in his name on the inside title page. Designer, Louise Fili.

top
Logo for Au Café, New York, NY.
Designer, Louise Fili; illustrator, Steven Guarnaccia.

above
Identity labels for Bartlett
Maine Estate Winery,
Gouldsboro, ME. These are
from a series of 18 different
labels for Bartlett fruit wines.
Designer, Louise Fili.

left
Menu design for Picholine,
a French Provençal restaurant, New York, NY.
Designer, Louise Fili;
illustrator, Anthony Russo.

right
Identity system for Candle
Cafe, a vegetarian restaurant,
New York, NY. The menu,
business card, letterhead
and envelope each use a
different engraving from a
vintage seed catalog.
Designer, Louise Fili.

far right
Packaging for Grafton
Goodjam, Grafton, VT.
From a series of nine
different gourmet vinegars.
Designer, Louise Fili.

below
Planting package and pot
for El Paso Chile Co.,
El Paso, TX.
Designer and copywriter,
Louise Fili.

FLORIBUNDA

EVERYTHING YOU NEED TO PLANT

contains:
potting soil,
liner, & five
hand-selected
bulbs of

the finest &
largest variety
imported
from
Holland

PAPERWHITES

above
Logo for Crawford Doyle
Booksellers, New York, NY.
Designer, Louise Fili;
illustrator, Anthony Russo.

above left
A Woman's Book of Days
and A Literary Book of
Days, Crown Publishing,
New York, NY.
Designer, Louise Fili; artist,
Rockwell Kent.

left
Carta Italiana, boxed note
cards featuring images from
Italian orange wrappers
for Chronicle Books,
San Francisco, CA.
Designer, Louise Fili;
illustrator, Melanie Parks.

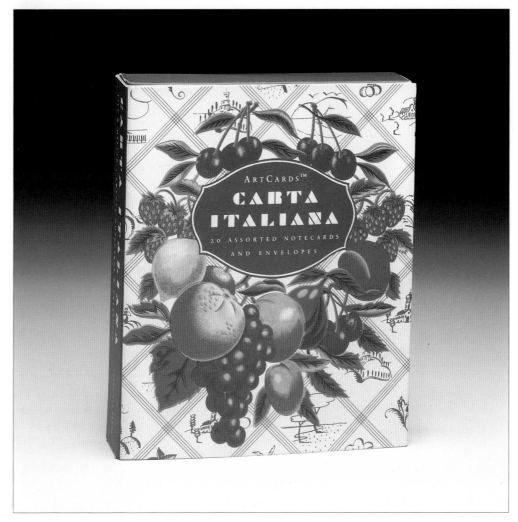

Michael Ian Kaye

Principal: Michael Ian Kaye
Year Founded: any minute...
Size of Firm: 1
Key Clients: Beacon Press,
City Bakery, The Dial Press,
Ecco Press, Farrar, Straus
and Giroux, HarperCollins,
Houghton Mifflin,
International Typeface
Corperation, Knopf, Simon
& Schuster, W.W. Norton,
Warner Books.

423 Atlantic Avenue
Brooklyn, NY 11217
718 522 0226

ichael Ian Kaye views each project as a logic puzzle, assessing not only the sum of the parts, but the individual merits of each component and its relationship to each other both visually and contextually. As Art Director of Farrar, Straus and Giroux, Kaye provides a consistent vision by focusing on conceptual thinking reinforced by meticulous craft. Provocation of thought becomes a driving force behind what at first glance appears to be understated, elegant studies in composition and form. Fascinated by the layering and interweaving of ideas and images, Kaye is concerned with seeing the forest through the trees—always keeping the goal of communication in mind.

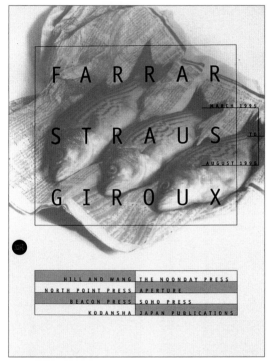

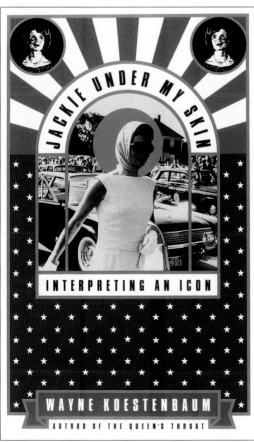

above
Catalog cover for Farrar, Straus and Giroux, New York, NY. The logo consists of three fish.
Designer, Michael Ian Kaye; photography, Melissa Hayden.

right
Book jacket for *Jackie Under My Skin*, interpreting an icon by Wayne Kostenbaum, for Farrar, Straus and Giroux. Designer, Michael Ian Kaye; photography, courtesy of AP/Wide World Photos.

left
Michael Ian Kaye.
Photography,
Ray Charles White.

Cover and three spreads
for the quarterly journal of
graphic design and digital
media, *U&lc*, International
Type Face Corporation,
New York, NY.
Designer, Michael Ian Kaye;
photography,
Melissa Hayden.

below
Book jacket for *Elizabeth*, A
Biography of Britain's Queen,
Farrar, Straus and Giroux.
Designer, Michael Ian Kaye;
photography, Cecil Beaton.

right
Book jacket for *Flesh and Blood*, Farrar, Straus and Giroux, New York, NY. The story is about a dysfunctional family. Designer, Michael Ian Kaye; photography, Melissa Hayden.

middle
Book jacket for *Mysterious Skin*, a gay, coming-of-age novel by Scott Heim, Harper-Collins, New York, NY. Designer, Michael Ian Kaye; art director, Joseph Montebello; photography, Melissa Hayden.

far right
Book jacket for *Lenin's Brain*, Farrar, Straus and Giroux. Designer, Michael Ian Kaye; art director, Doris Janowitz.

right
Book jacket for *Crash* and *Concrete Island*, two novels involving cars and sex in the future by J.G. Ballard, Farrar, Straus and Giroux. Designer, Michael Ian Kaye; photography, Melissa Hayden.

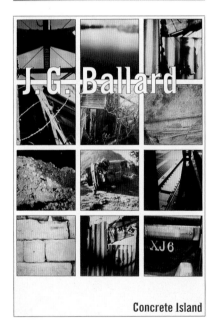

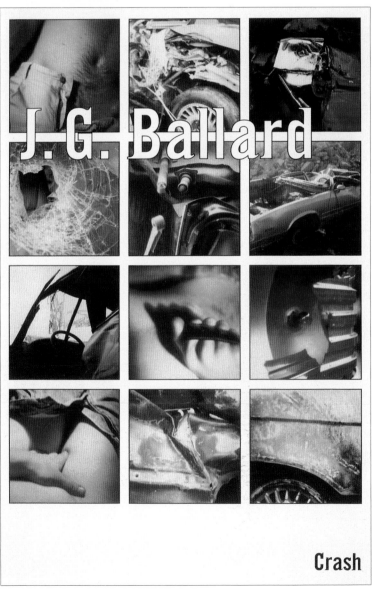

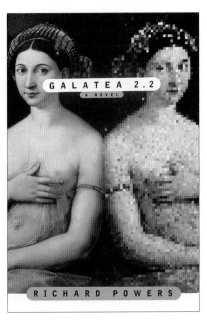

left to right
Book jacket for *The World is Round*, Farrar, Straus and Giroux.
Designer, Michael Ian Kaye; photography, Ray Lego.

Book cover for *Galatea 2.2*, a novel about love, art and technology, Farrar, Straus and Giroux.
Designer, Michael Ian Kaye; painting, Raphael Santi.

Book jacket for *The Marks of Birth*, Farrar, Straus and Giroux.
Designer, Michael Ian Kaye; photography, Melissa Hayden.

left to right
Book jacket for *The Burning*, a novel written from several viewpoints during a riot in Los Angeles, The Dial Press, New York, NY.
Designer/Illustrator, Michael Ian Kaye.

Book jacket for *Breaking Free*, a love story between an American diplomat and a Russian scientist. The backwards "R" in Cyrillic means "I". Farrar, Straus and Giroux.
Designer, Michael Ian Kaye.

Book jacket for *Bastard out of Carolina*, E.P. Dutton, New York, NY.
Designer, Michael Ian Kaye; art director, Neil Stuart; photography, Dorothea Lange.

left to right
Book jacket for *Making Modernism: Picasso and the Creation of the Market for Modern Art*, Farrar, Straus and Giroux.
Designer, Michael Ian Kaye; photography, Cecil Beaton.

Book jacket for *While England Sleeps*, an unorthodox gay love story that takes place in England during the 1930s, Viking, New York, NY.
Designer, Michael Ian Kaye; art director, Neil Stuart.

Book jacket for *The Bird Artist*, Farrar Straus & Giroux.
Designer, Michael Ian Kaye; illustrator, Ruth Marten.

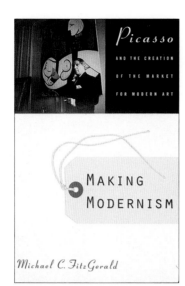

left to right
Book jacket for *Lush Life: A Biography of Billy Strayhorn*, Farrar, Straus and Giroux.
Designer, Michael Ian Kaye.

Book jacket for *U2 at the End of the World*, The Delacorte Press, New York, NY.
Designer, Michael Ian Kaye; photography, Anton Corbjin.

Book jacket for *The Death of Satan*, Farrar, Straus and Giroux. The design speaks of the demise of the concept of evil in American society.
Designer, Michael Ian Kaye.

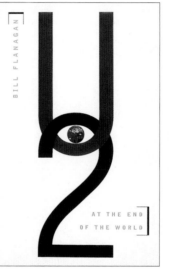
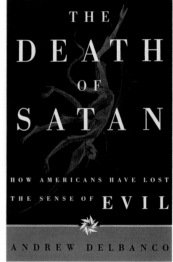

left to right
Book jacket for *Scar Tissue*, a novel about a mother with Alzheimers disease, Farrar, Straus and Giroux.
Designer, Michael Ian Kaye; photography, Michael McLaughlin.

Book jacket for *The Snarling Citizen*, essays by Barbara Ehrenreich, Farrar, Straus and Giroux.
Designer/Illustrator, Michael Ian Kaye.

Book jacket for *Konfidenz*, a novel about a mysterious love relationship, by Ariel Dorfman, Farrar, Straus and Giroux.
Designer, Michael Ian Kaye; photography, Melissa Hayden.

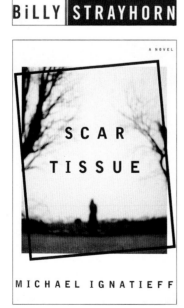

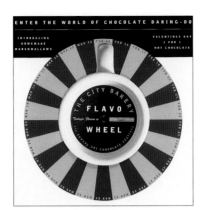

left and below
Poster design and calendar
of events for he City
Bakery's Hot Chocolate
Festival, New York, NY.
Design/Photography,
Michael Ian Kaye.

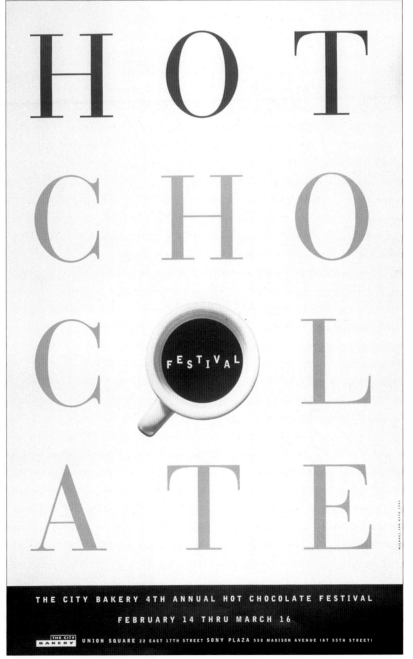

above
Book jacket for *Remarkable
Unspeakable New York*, a
collection of lively essays
about New York by major
literary figures, Beacon Press,
Boston, MA.
Designer, Michael Ian Kaye;
art director, Sara Eisenman;
photography, Rudy Burkhardt.

Mirko Ilić

Principals: Mirko Ilić
Year Founded: 1995
Size of Firm: 2
Key Clients: New York
Times, Rizzoli, Universe
Publishing, Sony, Time
Inc., PBC International,
Random House, MTV,
Golden Globe Awards,
Saunders Publishing.

207 East 32nd Street
New York, NY 10016
212 481 9737

Mirko Ilić builds his work on a foundation of intelligence, style and self-assurance—wielding illustration and design, knowledge of history and world affairs, and deep awareness of graphic art and technology. With a flexibility borne of spirited perception and consummate skill, he manages to take his work seriously without taking himself too seriously. "Mirko Ilić is a designer who draws and an illustrator who thinks," noted Milton Glaser. "...he is both incredibly stubborn and remarkably open-minded." Whether a magazine cover, newspaper layout, illustration, computer animation or book design, his work is unified by layered meaning and visual wit, showing equal reverence for both initial impact and sustained reflection—a combination of intelligence, style and self-assurance that maintains Ilić's foundation.

above and left
Poster and CD package design for Buldozer, a Slovenian band on Helidon Records. Noć, the title of the band's album, means night. Photography, Rajko Bizjak.

far left
Logo for Koncept Records, locoated in Zagreb, Croatia.

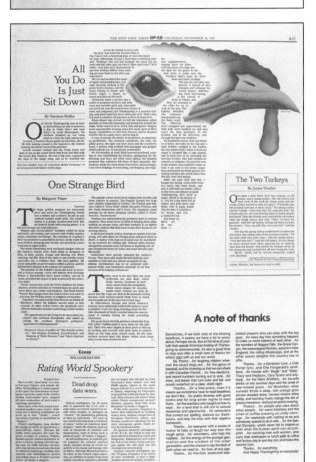

Design for the OP-ED section of the *New York Times*. "The Power of Laugh," illustration by Ruth Marten. "One Strange Bird," illustration by Milan Trenc. "The A.D.L. Under Fire" and "Russia Comes Apart," illustrations by Mirko Ilić. Art Director/Designer, Ilić.

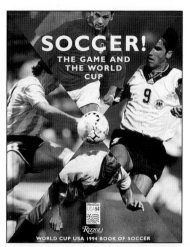

Book about the 1994 soccer
world cup for Rizzoli.
Art Director/Designer,
Mirko Ilić.

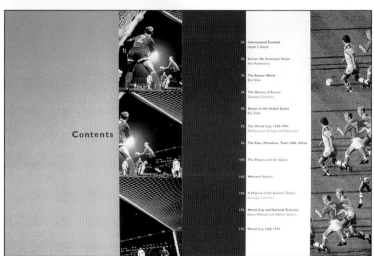

Contents

18. International Football
Joseph S. Blatter

20. Soccer: An American Vision
Alan Rothenberg

24. The Soccer World
Elio Trifari

36. The History of Soccer
Giuseppe Castelnovo

50. Soccer in the United States
Elio Trifari

52. The World Cup, 1930–1994
Pierfrancesco Archetti and Fabio Licari

86. The Fans, Maradona, Team USA, Africa

105. The Players and the Game

160. Women's Soccer

166. A History of the Game's Tactics
Giuseppe Castelnovo

170. World Cup and National Statistics
Gianni Mancuso and Alfonso Spedaro

176. World Cup USA 1994

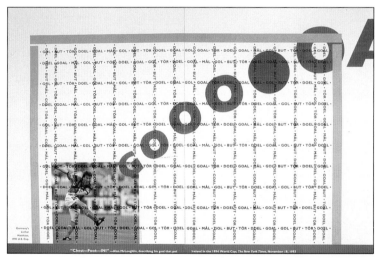

Bicycle kicks

Book of fine art portraits
of Marylin Monroe and
Elvis Presley for Rizzoli,
New York, NY.
Art Director/Designer,
Mirko Ilić.

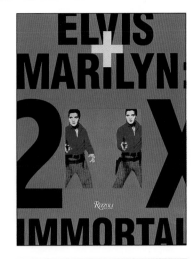

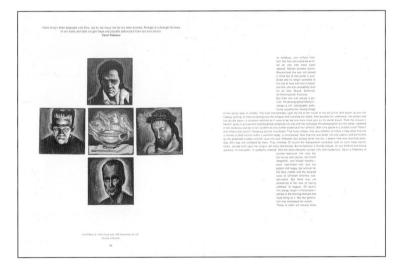

far right
Newspaper advertisement
for Mistique Papers.
Illustrator, Mirko Ilić;
designers, Pentagram, New
York; publisher, Champion
International.

right
Illustration for the OP-ED
section of the *New York
Times*, titled "Gulf War."
Illustrator, Mirko Ilić;
designer, Michael Valenti.

bottom right
Illustration for *Upper &
Lower Case* magazine, titled
"Origin of the letter 'R'. "
Illustrator, Mirko Ilić;
designer, WBMG Inc.

bottom right
Cover illustration for the
*New York Times Book
Review*, titled "What Fairy
Tales Mean."
Illustrator, Mirko Ilić;
designer, Steven Heller.

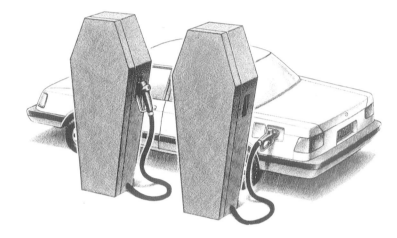

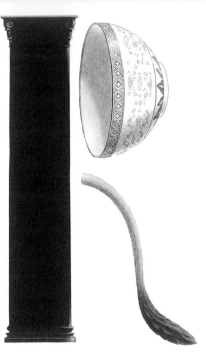

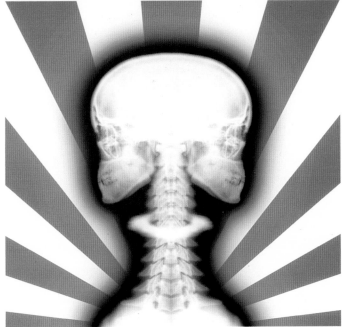

far left
Illustration for the *New York Times Book Review*, titled "The Havoc in Yugoslavia." Illustrator, Mirko Ilić; designer, Steven Heller.

left
Illustration for the *New York Times Book Review*, titled "Battered Housewives." Illustrator, Mirko Ilić; designer, Steven Heller.

bottom left
Illustration for the *New York Times Book Review*, titled "Hiroshima's Legacy." Illustrator, Mirko Ilić; designer, Steven Heller.

bottom
Illustration for the *New York Times Book Review*, titled "How to Recognize Shakespeares of Our Time." Illustrator, Mirko Ilić; designer, Steven Heller.

Number Seventeen

Principals: Emily Oberman,
Bonnie Siegler
Year Founded: 1993
Size of Firm: 7
Key Clients: ABC
Television, America Online,
Chronicle Books,
Cole + Weber, God's Love
We Deliver, Independent
Television Service, Isaac
Mizrahi, MTV Networks,
New Line Cinema,
Saturday Night Live,
The Red Hot Organization,
WGBH.

285 West Broadway
Room 650
New York, NY 10013
212 966 9395

Number Seventeen's work is always driven by the idea. Sometimes it's funny, sometimes it's serious, sometimes it's scary—and oftentimes it's completely different from what the client expects. Founded by Emily Oberman and Bonnie Siegler, Number Seventeen is a multi-disciplinary firm that works in the video, film, print and computer medium. The goal: to tackle work never tried before. Believing that good design solutions will, by definition, be beautiful—design should be inspired by its potential enjoyment rather than potential profit. By not operating with a "design for design's sake" philosophy, this approach helps to feed Number Seventeen's clever and well-thought design, the kind of design that keeps the firm's creators doing work they love.

right
A commercial that parodied the clear product craze, specifically the Crystal Pepsi spot, for Saturday Night Live, New York, NY. Designers, Emily Oberman and Bonnie Siegler; director, Jim Signorelli; writer, Dave Mandel.

below
Illustrated view of Number Seventeen's studio on a self-promotional postcard. In the tradition of the grand hotels of the 1940's, the firm wanted to share their "home away from home" with friends and colleagues. Designers, Emily Oberman and Bonnie Siegler; illustrator, Arline Simon.

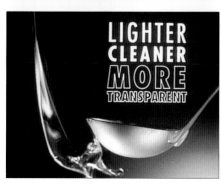

right
From left, top row: Bonnie
Siegler and Emily Oberman;
middle row: Matthew
Jacobson, Anne Mullen
and David Israel;
bottom row: Robby Fahey
and Ramsey Hong;
not pictured: Keira Alexandra
and Nomi Joy Siegler.
Photography,
Ray Charles White.

below
One in a series of advertisements for VH-1, New York,
NY. The design group infu-
riated the Catholic Church
by showing the two most
famous Madonnas together.
Stories on major news networks and the front page of
the *New York Post* brought
quick attention to the then
month-old office.
Designers, Emily Oberman
and Bonnie Siegler.

below right
Identity program and on-air
broadcast logo for ABC
Daytime, New York, NY.
The new logo showed ABC
and Daytime at the same
time. With an already strong,
established logo to work with,
identifications were created
that introduced the new logo
in a variety of ways, such as
this "Stretch" identity.
Designers, Emily Oberman,
Bonnie Siegler and
Matthew Jacobson

above
Double X, an encyclopedia
for the "3rd Wave" of feminism, for Agincourt Press,
New York, NY. Instead of
using the traditional symbol,
the mirror of Venus, a double
x was created as a modern
feminist symbol. The book
is a reference guide that helps
define feminism today—
from Androgyny-to-
Wonderbra.
Designers, Emily Oberman,
Bonnie Siegler and Eric Zim;
artist, Portia Munson.

below
Number Seventeen's
business card.
Designers, Emily Oberman,
Bonnie Siegler and
Matthew Jacobson.

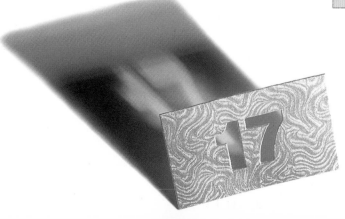

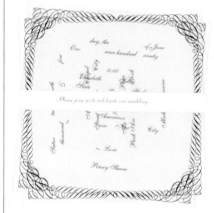

above
Car commercial parody of
the original Subaru campaign
for Saturday Night Live.
Designers, Emily Oberman
and Bonnie Siegler;
director, Jim Signorelli;
writer, Dave Mandel.

left
Wedding invitation for
Penny Shane and Michael
Tomaino, New York, NY.
It was created as a twist on
a traditional wedding invi-
tation, while acting as a
metaphor for marriage.
Designers, Emily Oberman
and Bonnie Siegler.

above
Thirty-second television
commercial for
Cole+Weber, Seattle, WA.
The type treatment was
designed to support the
message without over-
whelming the images.
Designers, Emily Oberman
and Bonnie Siegler;
director, Matt Mahurin.

right
"Please Stand By," spot
for VH-1 let the viewers
know that the channel
is experiencing technical
difficulties while using
humor for a normally dry
piece of information.
Designer, Bonnie Siegler.

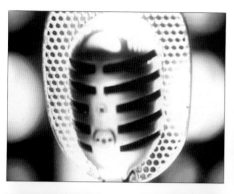

left
Identity for Berlin, Wright,
Cameron, New York, NY.
The new, young ad agency
needed to convey they were
hip as well as buttoned up
and professional. The business card is unique because
the employees were asked
to pick the text, which
conveyed a hint of the
bearer's personality.
Designers, Emily Oberman,
Bonnie Siegler and
Matthew Jacobson.

above
Condé Naste commercial
for Berlin, Wright, Cameron.
The objective was to remind
people that in the wake of
the current technological
revolution, the most important element is content.
Designers, Emily Oberman
and Bonnie Siegler;
director, Mark Cappos;
writer, Scott Burns.

below
Identity program and
on-air broadcast logo for
ABC Daytime. The
"Sunrise" identity.
Designers, Emily Oberman,
Bonnie Siegler and
Matthew Jacobson.

below
Number Seventeen sticker.
Designers, Emily Oberman,
Bonnie Siegler and
Matthew Jacobson;
inspector, Momus.

left
Opening sequence to
The United States of Poetry,
a five-part series airing on
public television for
Washington Square Films,
New York, NY. The
Independent Television
Service funded series is a
portrait of America guided
by the words and voices of
over 60 American poets.
Designers, Emily Oberman
and Bonnie Siegler;
director, Mark Pellington.

below center
Interstitial element entitled
"The American Dream,"
one part of the series for
United States of Poetry.
Because excerpts from the
poems all relate to politics
and society, iconic American
imagery combined with a
target was used to subvert
its traditional meanings.
Designers, Emily Oberman
and Bonnie Siegler;
director, Mark Pellington.

above
Invitation for the Beaux
Arts Ball, the Architectural
League's biggest annual
event, New York, NY.
Come as yourself—or your
favorite building.
Designers, Emily Oberman,
Bonnie Siegler and
Matthew Jacobson.

below
Television campaign for
WXRT Radio, Chicago, IL.
The commercial helps to
differentiate WXRT from
Top 40 radio stations, and
tries to show a musical
stream of consciousness.
Designer, Emily Oberman;
writer, Scott Burns;
director of photography,
Tom Richmond.

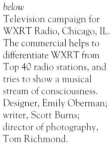

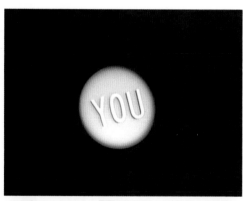

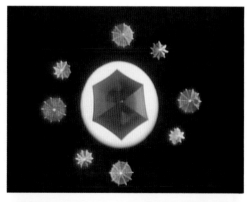

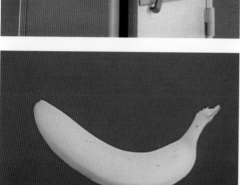

left
Public service announcement for the Red Hot Organization, New York, NY. The packaging and interstitial elements for the MTV special, showcasing the album, "No Alternative" used the visual language of MTV to convey to teens the idea that "Safe Sex is Hot Sex."
Designers, Emily Oberman and Bonnie Siegler.

left and above
A monthly program guide for QVC, West Chester, PA. The *TV Guide*-like magazine doubled as a catalog and contained editorial information.
Designers, Emily Oberman and Bonnie Siegler.

right
Identity program and on-air broadcast logo for ABC Daytime, inspired by Busby Berkeley.
Designers, Emily Oberman, Bonnie Siegler and Matthew Jacobson.

below
Number Seventeen's plaque design in Spanish.
Designers, Emily Oberman and Bonnie Siegler; fabricator, Quill.

Reprinted from
Graphic Design: New York 2
Printed in Hong Kong

Cockroach photo by
Tom SCHIERLITZ
212.431.4195

The rest by
James VICTORE
212.925.6862

*Any resemblance, overtly or
otherwise, to any overpopulated,
overcommercialized,
misgoverned island to the right
of New Jersey, is purely
unintentional.*

NO PARKING

TRIBORO BRIDGE

HARLEM
Take the "A" train

The melting pot theory has failed. Here's proof. The pizza guy doesn't even deliver here.

GEORGE WASHINGTON BRIDGE

UPPER EAST SIDE
Roughly 14th Street to Nova Scotia, East of Fifth Avenue

One train? Are you kidding? Rumor has it that people actually live up here, though no one would ever publicly admit this. The ASPCA is up here (*everyone should have a kitten*), as well as the incomparable chocolate bread from Ecce Panis. There are possibly some museums, too.

57TH STREET
NYC's newest mall

Niketown©, the Disney© Store, the Warner Bros©. Store, all it needs now is a Fuddruckers© and one of those stores that make really huge cookies ... Put a roof on it, it's done.

TIMES SQUARE
Broadway from 42nd St. to 47th St.

Totally live! Totally nude! A good place to find your wretched refuse yearning to breath free. This area is a big draw for tourists, although no one knows why. Neon lighted billboards, gaudy storefronts, it's beautiful here at night, especially if you can't read. Feel free to play 3-card monty with the locals. Don't forget to try a dirty-water hot dog or a fried shrimp dish from one of the cheerful street vendors, *they're good for you.*

LINCOLN TUNNEL

MANHATTAN BRIDGE

LITTLE-CHINA-ITALY-TOWN
Borders change daily

Tacky restaurants, terrible food and bad service, unless of course you're related. Great for knick-knacks, chatchkas, t-shirts, cultural clichés and sfogliatella. P.S. Please don't ask for "flied lice" in a Chinese restaurant, it's terribly rude.

HOLLAND TUNNEL

WALL STREET
The intersection of Fear and Greed

Home of the chiggers, lice, vermin and rabid dogs that run the world economy. Hide your wallet and watch your back, this is where the big crime happens. Nice place to visit, though. Don't miss Battery Park City, also known as the "white projects".

SoHo
SOuth of HOuston Street, but North of Canal Street, get it?

Death by tourism. The shops and galleries this area became known for are being replaced by far too many "chic" restaurants and mega retail chains. Check out the nouveau-riche-cappuccino-sucking-Hell's Angels-wanna-be's and the roving gangs of slow-moving, shopping-bag-toting Europeans. Also known as the "Bridge and Tunnel" plague, this atrophy is now spreading to Tribeca (*The TRIangle BElow CAnal, get it?*).

BROOKLYN BRIDGE

STATEN ISLAND FERRY

BROOKLYN BATTERY TUNNEL

$0 $50 $500 $5K $50K

Parham Santana Design

Principals/
Creative Directors: John
Parham, Maruchi Santana
Year Founded: 1985
Size of Firm: 10
Key Clients: CBS/Fox Video,
Guess? Eyewear, MTV
Networks, NBC, Scholastic
Inc., Sony Electronics Inc.,
USA Networks.

7 West 18th Street
New York, NY 10011
212 645 7501

 arham Santana, unlike many design firms, doesn't resist labels. In fact, the firm wears them proudly. Its designers created six mailing labels that doubled as mini, self-promotional advertisements. Messages such as "Treat yourself to the very best," and "We care if it's square," do more than reveal the hip edge and sly humor that pervades much of the firm's work; it's also a hint of the visual, verbal and marketing sensibilites that drive the husband-wife partnership of John Parham and Maruchi Santana. The two met while graduate students at Pratt Institute, however, much of their inspiration comes not from academia, but from a commitment to marketing and research. Parham Santana believes that learning the market and positioning the product makes design more relevant, and allows for a range of solutions. Their belief that design can be both beautiful and smart keeps opening doors to top clients in the entertainment, information and licensing industries. In Parham Santana's case, labels do help.

above
Packaging for NBA
Video; CBS/Fox Video,
New York, NY. Targeted
to a teenage, male demo-
graphic, the package doubles
as a mini-poster with graphics and colors that represent
the convergence of sports
and entertainment.
Art Directors, Benjamin
Niles and Lori Reinig.

left
Packaging and watch
design for Coca-Cola
Watches; SMH, New
York, NY. A line of 50's-
inspired watches uses
Coca-Cola's archival
imagery as an American
standard to project quality.
Art Director,
Maruchi Santana.

left
left
Left to right: John Parham,
Millie Hsi, Maruchi Santana
and Rick Tesoro.
Photography,
Ray Charles White.

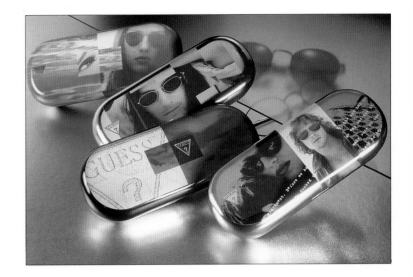

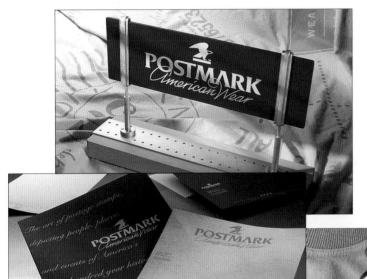

above
Guess? Eyewear collectible
tins for Viva International
Group, Fairfield, NJ. The
packaging doubles as point-
of-sale display and helps
distinguish Guess? in a
crowded eyewear market.
Art Directors, Millie Hsi
and Lori Reinig.

below
Harley Davidson Eyewear
packaging for Viva Inter-
national Group, Fairfield,
NJ. Designed to attract a
new consumer without
alienating the die-hard
Harley owner.
Art Director, Millie Hsi.

above and right
Identity for American
Eagle Apparel Group,
New York, NY. Postmark
American Wear is an
exclusive collection of
casual and active sportswear
inspired by stamp graphics
from 200-years of U.S.
Postal Service Archives.
Art Director, Rick Tesoro.

top to bottom
• Image Display
• Corporate Stationery
• Hangtags
Using utilitarian materials
and familiar colors, the
firm created a marriage of
tradition and freshness
throughout the Postmark
program. The concept of
'collectibility' is reinforced
through hangtags,
dedicated to limited edition
Postmark products.

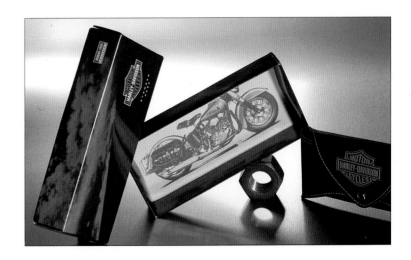

left
Media sales kit for VH1,
New York, NY. Since the
music channel was reposi-
tioned as "VH1: Music First,"
the kit was developed as
"The Source"—the ultimate
guide to VH1 and music.
The Source contains pro-
gramming, demographics,
quotes, inside information,
postcards and a positioning
statement to create a rich
'everything music' message.
Art Director, Millie Hsi;
copywriter,
Diana Amsterdam.

below
Nickelodeon and Flintstones
computer accessory kit for
Brain Works, Port Wash-
ington, NY. A unique,
wedge-shaped, picture
window package for today's
inventory-rich, sales-staff
poor stores.
Art Director, Millie Hsi.

above left
Poster series for VH1
Fashion and Music Awards;
VH1/MTV Networks, New
York, NY. Part of a nation-
wide campaign that also
included windshield posters,
banners and print advertising.
Creative Director,
Dean Lubensky, VH1;
art director, Millie Hsi.

above
Sales system for VH1.
Art Director, Dean
Lubensky; VH1 off-air
creative designers, Paula
Kelly and Lori Reinig.

below
Sales promotion kit for
Grand Slam Tennis; USA
Networks, New York, NY.
Creative Director, Elisa
Feinman, USA;
art director, Lori Reinig.

bottom left
Consumer packaging for
Nickelodeon Electronic
Product; Long Hall
Technologies, Inc.,
Hicksville, NY.
Art Director, Rick Tesoro.

right
Product literature for high-
end automotive stereo
systems; Sony Electronics
Inc., Park Ridge, NJ.
Designed like a sophisticated
users manual, the emphasis
is on product and lifestyle.
Art Directors, Parham
Santana; copywriter,
Glenn Estersohn.

below
Packaging and components
for "Safe Schools/Safe
Streets;" Scholastic Inc.,
New York, NY. Designed to
be credible and have 'kid
appeal' without stereotyping
any age or racial group.
Programs were developed by
Scholastic to constructively
deal with and initiate dialogue
about problems involving
today's youth.
Creative Director, Ellen
Jacob, Scholastic; art director,
Rick Tesoro.

Meet the inventor of SAT test prep.

Our venerable founder, **Stanley** H. Kaplan, the original whiz kid, the first and only true braintrainer. **Stanley** may not wear the latest hightops and we've never seen him in baggies. But when it comes to the SAT, **Stanley** knows the score. **Stanley**, like all true brains, believes that there's no substitute for actual knowledge. For real instruction. For deep strategy. For more than 50 years, **Stanley**

and his in-the-trenches teachers have **raised** scores. **Stanley** may have taught **your** mother. **Stanley** has stood behind **over 2 million students** – more than all other test preppers, combined! Come in and catch the **Stanley** spirit of test prep. **Train your brain.**

Stanley Says: "It is incumbent upon you at this juncture to investigate further the myriad benefits of our SAT prep courses including the inimitable SAT Prep Plus and the exceptional SAT Challenge."

In other words: *CALL US NOW.* To sign up or for more info, dial:
1-800-KAP-TEST

KAPLAN
The answer to the test question.

left/right
Kaplan is a company that sells test preparation. The challenge was to turn this company's reputation around and get its message across to a younger audience. The "Meet Stanley Campaign" features founder Stanley H. Kaplan as "the original whiz kid" talking "Stanley talk" (lots of big words) and looking exceptionally scholarly.
Art Director, Rick Stermole; copywriter, Diana Amsterdam.

below
Poster series for Kaplan, New York, NY. Kaplan Rules were developed as both a leadership statement and as the 10 rules, or principles, for successful test taking.
Art Director, Alexander Knowlton; copywriter, Diana Amsterdam.

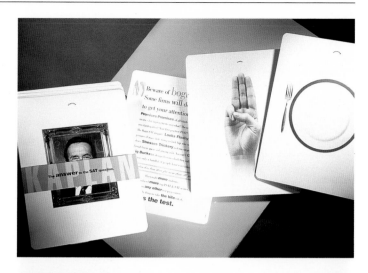

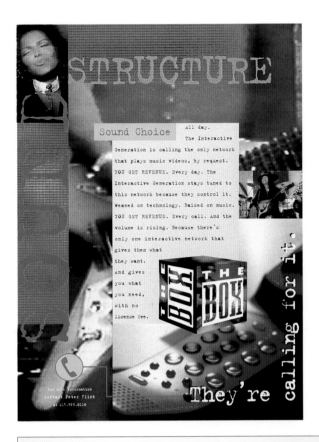

far left
THE BOX "Sound Structure" advertising campaign for Video Jukebox Network, Miami, FL. The campaign repositions THE BOX and defines its audience: "The Interactive Generation." Art Director, Rick Tesoro; copywriter, Diana Amsterdam

left
Sales kit. A die-cut throughout the brochure reveals an image of a VCR control button. As each page is turned, the viewer builds the mission statement: "Music Television You Control." Art Director, Rick Tesoro; copywriter, Diana Amsterdam.

left
Video packaging for VH1; a nineties look back at the icons of the 1970s. Art Director, Dean Lubensky; VH1 off-air creative designers, Rick Tesoro and Paula Kelly.

below
Video catalog for BMG Video, New York, NY. A collage of the Bertelsmann Building in Times Square positions the company as a creative resource within a media powerhouse. Creative Director, Jodi Rovin; BMG Video designer, Ron Anderson.

Paul Davis Studio

Principal: Paul Davis
Year Founded: 1984
Size of Firm: 5
Key Clients: The Amicus
Journal, Bay Street Theatre,
Benedictine, Columbia
University, CUNY,
Fukuoka City Bank, Harper
Collins, Hewlett Packard,
Mobil Corporation, MTV,
Time Inc., Unite!

14 East 4th Street
New York, NY 10012
212 420 8789

aul Davis Studio forges identities that capture attention. A painter, digital artist and photographer as well as a graphic designer, Paul Davis has created powerful images for institutions, products, books and magazines. Various cultural projects and events include Joseph Papp's New York Shakespeare Festival, WNCN radio, the Hampton Classic, the Big Apple Circus and Bénédictine. Letting passion and invention distinguish his work, he has served as founding art director for two magazines and a museum, and has produced murals, film animation, sculptures and billboards for a wide variety of clients.

left
Special illustrated holiday packaging for Bénédictine, Paris, France. The image was originally designed for a poster and exhibition in Paris. (Application of art by Bénédictine).
Illustrator, Paul Davis.

left
Identity and application for the creation of a new union under which the Amalgamated Clothing Workers union and the Ladies' Garment Workers union merged into Unite! (the Union of Needletrades, Industrial and Textile Employees), for the AFL-CIO, CLC, New York, NY. The goal was to create a modern look to represent two of the most progressive American unions.
Designer, Paul Davis.

left and opposite page bottom
1993 and 1996 season
poster for Bay Street Theatre,
Sag Harbor, NY.
Design/Illustration,
Paul Davis.

below
Invitation and booklet
design for "High Times,"
a benefit for the New York
Shakespeare Festival.
Designers, Paul Davis and
Mariana Ochs.

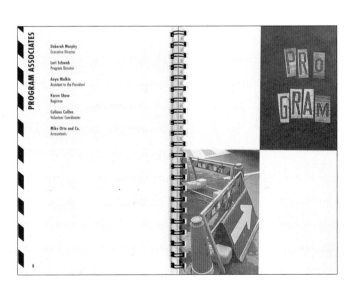

far left and left
Program booklet and poster
design for IDCA, the 43rd
International Design
Conference in Aspen, CO.
The theme of the confer-
ence was "Reconstruction
Ahead," using elements of
building and construction.
Designers, Paul Davis and
Lisa Mazur.

WRITERS' VOICES

SELECTED FROM

THE JOY LUCK CLUB

AMY TAN

NEW WRITERS' VOICES

SNApSHOTS

Two Stories by New Writers

NEW WRITERS' VOICES

BARS COMING NEAR

left
Series of book cover designs for Literacy Volunteers of New York, NY. Designers, Paul Davis and Lisa Mazur.

Series of promotional books designed for Nexus, an international architecture project in Fukuoka, Japan created by the great Japanese architect Arata Isozaki and six young architects: Oscan Tusquets, Christian de Portzampare, Osamu Ishiyama, Mark Mack, Rem Koolhaas and Steven Holl. The books include presentations and photographs of the projects in progress. Designers, Paul Davis and Mariana Ochs; editorial, Myrna Davis; illustrator, Philippe Weisbecker.

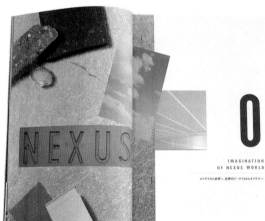

0

IMAGINATION OF NEXUS WORLD

ネクサスから世界へ、世界のアーチストからネクサスへ。

far left
Logo for "Magazine 2000,"
an article on the future of
interactive magazines for
U&lc Magazine, ITC
International Typeface
Company, New York, NY.
Designers, Paul Davis,
Lisa Mazur and
Chalkley Calderwood.

left and below
Guest art direction (cover
and spread) on *U&lc
Magazine*, an international
journal of typography and
design. The goal with the
20th Anniversary issue was
to edit 20 years of the magazine's work and come up
with the cream of the crop.
"The real design challenge
for us was to take all of this
old, rich material, and show
it in a fresh, new way."
Designers, Paul Davis,
Lisa Mazur and
Chalkley Calderwood.

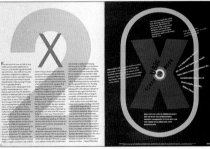

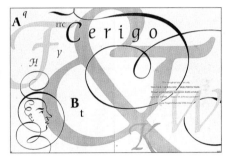

left
Book cover design for
Columbia University Press,
New York, NY.
Art Director, Paul Davis;
designer, Chalkley
Calderwood.

left
Image for the 1994 MTV Music Awards book with the theme of "free your mind," for MTV Networks, New York, NY. Illustrator, Paul Davis.

bottom left
Poster design for the Bay Street Theatre Festival, Sag Harbour, NY. One of an ongoing series from 1992 to the present. Designers, Paul Davis and Chalkley Calderwood.

below middle
Compact disc cover design for Milan Entertainment, New York, NY. Illustrator, Paul Davis.

bottom middle
Poster for an exhibition, "Paul Davis: The Uses of Style," at the Visual Arts Museum, New York, NY. Designer, Paul Davis.

below
Poster for the Long Island Association for AIDS Care, East Hampton, NY. The poster advertises a Fourth of July benefit exhibition for the program. Designer, Paul Davis.

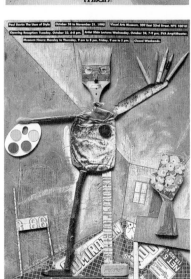

below left
Poster design for Mobil
Mystery Theatre, New York,
NY. Mystery is a series
shown on PBS and is spon-
sored by Mobil.
Designer, Paul Davis.

bottom left
Design and cover illustration
for 92nd Street Y, New York,
NY. The catalog was created
to replace three separate
brochures. "Our goal was
to give the program the
feeling of a University."
Designer, Paul Davis.

below right
Cover illustration for
CUNY Freshman
Admissions catalog, Long
Island City, NY. The covers
emphasize the diversity of
the student body and the
multiple CUNY campuses.
Designer, Paul Davis.

bottom right
Brochure design for
Columbia University,
New York, NY.
Designers, Paul Davis and
Brooke Meinhardt.

below
Poster design and illustration
for "Secret Friends," a
surreal and disorienting film
by Dennis Potter, for
Geisler and Roberdeau
New York, NY.
Designer, Paul Davis.

bottom
Cover design and illustration
for the *Amicus Journal*, New
York, NY; a publication of
the Natural Resources
Defenses Council. This is
one of an ongoing series
from 1993 to present.
Designers, Paul Davis and
Brook Meinhardt.

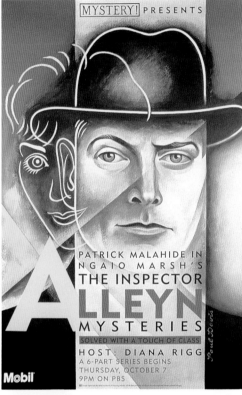

Pentagram

Principals: James Biber, Michael Bierut, Michael Gericke, Peter Harrison, Paula Scher, Woody Pirtle
Year Founded: 1978
Size of Firm: 45
Key Clients: American Institute of Architects, American Museum of Natural History, G.H. Bass & Co., Bausch & Lomb, Brooklyn Academy of Music, Disney Development Company, Mohawk Paper Mills, National Audubon Society, New York Times Magazine, Nine West, Texaco, United Technologies.

204 Fifth Avenue
New York, NY 10010
212.683.7000

entagram's New York office recently moved to its own building on Fifth Avenue, obscuring once and for all the image of a small outpost of a British firm. Now in its second generation of partner-principals, Pentagram New York continues to turn out an abundance of graphic and 3-D work that defies stylistic pigeonholing—except for the common threads of innovative thinking and exceptional production. Since the first edition of *Graphic Design: New York*, graphic designers Paula Scher and Michael Gericke have become partners in the Manhattan office, as well as architect James Biber. The combination has re-created in America the multi-disciplinary practice that has distinguished Pentagram in London since 1972. New branches in Austin, Texas and Hong Kong have further broadened the scope of the firm since 1991. Pentagram's partnership structure is the core of its strength—similar to a small, private firm, each partner offers individual expertise and intimate involvement with the client and the design process. But, like a large international firm, the group also maintains a sophisticated support structure and a deep network of resources. Clients, designers, and the projects—all benefit from the influence and stimulation of Pentagram's diverse design activities.

left
From left: Michael Bierut,
Michael Gericke, Paula
Scher, Peter Harrison
(front), James Biber and
Woody Pirtle.
Photography,
Ray Charles White.

Corporate identity and
architectural graphics program for the Minnesota
Children's Museum, St. Paul,
MN. Playing off the
Museum's dedication to
"hands on" activities, photographs of children's hands
were used throughout the
building. Combined with a
bright color palette and custom alphabet, the hands
point directions, count off
floor numbers, and hold
room identification icons.
The same images appear on
the Museum's stationery,
print material and, most
dramatically, on the new
downtown building's
facade—45-feet tall.
Design team, Michael
Bierut and Tracey
Cameron; photography,
Don F. Wong.

THE PUBLIC THEATER

Graphic identity for The Public Theater, New York, NY. Best known for producing the New York Shakespeare Festival in Central Park, The Public Theater is also one of the city's leading venus for new theatrical productions. Producer George C. Wolfe's ambition is to make the theater more *public*. This is achieved by enlarging the scope and diversity of its audience and promoting itself as streetwise, timely and accessible. Building on the undisciplined typography of the streetscape, the new program is active, unconventional, and with a twist of graffiti-like street-smarts. Design team: Paula Scher, Lisa Mazur, Ron Louie and Jane Mella.

above and center
An umbrella logo works in combination with a set of monogrammed roundels or stamps that identify the individual activities within the Public Theatre.

right
Graphics for the New York Shakespeare Festival in Central Park were derived from the all-type tradition of old-fashioned English theater announcements.

top
New interior signage for the theater lobby.

middle
The Public's bold, blocky visual language is reinterpreted for advertisements and other print materials.

opposite page
Public Theater production posters are based on graphic juxtapositions of photography and type. *Silence, Cunning, Exile* was loosely based on the life of photographer Diane Arbus. *The Diva is Dismissed* was Jenifer Lewis' one-woman show. Danny Hoch portrayed multiple personalities in *Some People*. A star-studded cast performed in Sam Shepard's cerebral play, *Simpatico*.

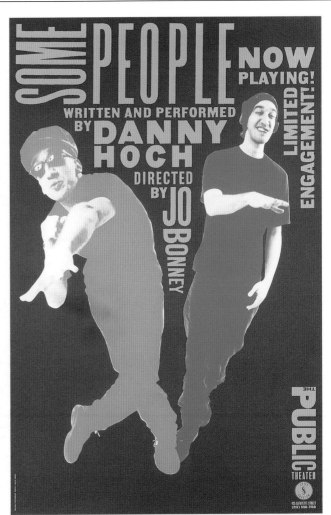

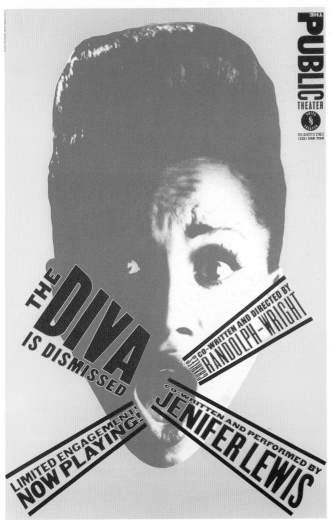

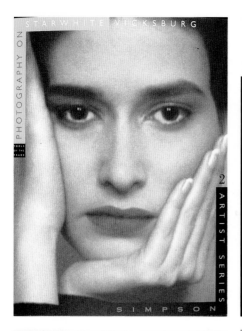

PHOTOGRAPHY ON STARWHITE VICKSBURG

TOOLS OF THE TRADE

2 ARTIST SERIES

SIMPSON

profiles

Before daguerreotype ushered in the age of photography in 1839, only the well-off could afford to have pictures of themselves. The camera changed all that. Inexpensive and easily obtained, photographs gave ordinary folks a means to create their family histories, even though the camera itself was too complex to manage on their Throughout the 19th century

From the 1920s to the '60s, Paul Strand created masterpieces using just two cameras, two lenses and commonplace darkroom techniques. But Strand embraced the evolving print technology to translate his original photographs into books and portfolio editions. His portrait of a young farmer is brought to life on soft white Archive vovr. Like the original, the tritone on the previous page seems carved from light and shadow.

still life
photo
graphy

objects

For photographers, still life has always been a vehicle for experimentation, a means to study texture, form and light in a controlled environment using subjects that won't walk away. In skillful hands, a simple pear, bell pepper or machine tool becomes monumental in scale. Objects can appear dramatic, powerful or sensuous with the right lighting, arrangement and styling. Designers have found

still life particularly useful because even the most ordinary products can be romanced by the camera to bring out a special quality. For viewers, these tantalizing, informative and sometimes provocative photographs delight the eye and stimulate the mind by providing a fresh appreciation for things we often take for granted. As much as photographers like to control every aspect of a still life, designers consider the shade of a paper key to enhancing an image. For that reason, Starwhite Vicksburg is offered in several subtle hues including creamy white Ivory. Here, *Starwhite Vicksburg Ivory* presents a pear still life, reproduced in 4-color process plus a touch plate of silver, 4-color process, and 4-color process prepared with a stochastic screen to show its versatility on press.

fashion
photo
graphy

It's amazing what just two colors can do. With this black-and-white photograph of supermodel Christie Brinkley created by legendary fashion photographer Francesco Scavullo, we used six different duotone combinations to show how an image can be transformed in mood and impact. Because the two colors often result in a third unexpected color, at the bottom of each page we provide a color bar and show the match colors used. The duotone comparison is presented on facing smooth and vellum pages of Tiara, which offers a brilliant white shade to capture tonal nuances and excellent formation to tightly register every detail.

archi
tectural
photo
graphy

landscape
photo
graphy

building

Majestic architecture—structures built from man's highest aspirations—has always been a favorite subject for photographers. Before cameras geared for non-professionals were introduced in the 1890s, many photographers specialized in scenic views of landmark buildings, eagerly collected as travel souvenirs. By the 1900s, black-and-white postcards printed by the thousands met the growing demand. Color film, introduced in the 1930s, was initially disdained by architectural photographers because

idday light, with its clean shadows and highlights, casts the terra cotta figures in sharp relief. On page 41, the effect is emphasized by the choice of colors in the tritone and Hi-Tech's brilliant white Tiara shade. The sheet's exceptional brightness reproduces color with sparkling clarity. Here, the linear pattern runs horizontally for textural variety.

earth & sky

Photographs of awesome wilderness panoramas, vast grasslands and intimate garden views have always had a special appeal. They offer relief from the pressures of urban life and remind us of nature's wondrous diversity. Used in brochures and annual reports, they can signify a commitment to responsible interaction with the environment.

American landscape photography has enjoyed a history as fascinating as the images themselves. Carleton E. Watkins was one of the first to capture land and cloud formations in one photograph. Through sophisticated printing techniques, he depicted the luminous meeting of earth and sky to convey the majestic beauty of the West. Images such as these were instrumental in Congress's decision to set aside entire regions as national parks. In this century, landscape

photographers have continued the tradition with images that stir the imagination and increase public awareness of ecological concerns. Many contemporary image-makers convey nature's splendor by zeroing in on details that express more than the sum of their parts. On *Starwhite Vicksburg Natural*, these attributes come forward even more harmoniously. Natural's warm white shade expresses the tone, texture and character of nature in a way that makes us respond to the landscape around us. In this section of overlapping pages, we demonstrate the versatility of Natural by providing a visual comparison of black-and-white reproductions. Natural maintains depth and detail, as shown here on its smooth and vellum finishes in various weights.

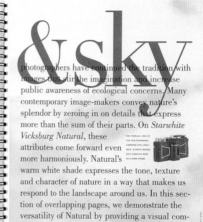

Series of paper promotions for the Simpson Paper Company, Seattle, WA. The "Tools of the Trade" series celebrates visual artists, their achievements and their instruments. For the target audience—graphic designers—the promotions needed to represent the highest level of visual and technical sophistication. This edition focused on the history, artifacts and heroes of photography. Layers of visual and textual information illuminate a brief history of the medium while demonstrating the tactile qualities of the Starwhite Vicksburg papers.
Design team: Woody Pirtle, John Klotnia and Ivette Montes de Oca.

Pushpin

Principal: Seymour Chwast
Year Founded: 1954
Size of Firm: 10
Key Clients: Addison
Wesley, American Express,
Diplomat Corporation,
El Paso Chili, Harry N.
Abrams, Hunter Douglas,
Mobil Oil, Mohawk Paper,
New York Times, Paul
Tracy Associates, Paul
Weiss Rifkind, Wharton &
Garrison, Time Warner.

18 East 16th Street
7th Floor
New York, NY 10003
212 255 6456
www.pushpin.com

Pushpin rode the crest of the graphic design wave in the 1960's—and ever since has captured the imagination of the world through the firm's refreshingly organic approach to design and illustration. Visual references are eclectic; connecting the fine art, cultural and literary movements of the 20th century while producing practical and innovative communication tools. The Pushpin Group's design is a celebration of humanity: content is conveyed through warmth, humor and an awareness of the gestalt, the universal timeless knowledge we share.

below left and below
One of seven brochures on the great design movements of the 20th century for Mohawk Paper Mills, Cohoes, NY. The brochure below, about the German Bauhaus, features a foldout of the primary faculty-designers from the movement. Examples of all aspects of design were gathered from various collections, including those of Pushpin and Steven Heller.
Designers, Seymour Chwast and Roxanne Slimak; writer/editor, Steven Heller.

left
Partners of Pushpin Group:
Seymour Chwast and
DK Holland.
Photography,
Ray Charles White.

Mark for the Bay Area
Children's Discovery
Museum, Sausalito, CA.
Designer, Seymour Chwast.

Mark for a publishing group
that produces promotional
brochures for photographers,
Solo Editions, New York, NY.
Designers, Seymour Chwast
and Greg Simpson.

Logo for a company that
markets wholesale quilt
products, Arch Quilts,
New York, NY.
Designers, Seymour Chwast
and William Bevington.

Identity for a pre-press
house, Lloyd & Germain,
Ltd., New York, NY.
Designers, Seymour Chwast
and William Bevington.

above
Children can create the
three-dimensional pets in
this book—produced by
Pushpin and published by
Harry N. Abrams,
New York, NY.
Designer/Illustrator,
Seymour Chwast.

right
Mr. Merlin and the Turtle,
Greenwillow Books, New
York, NY. It is a recent
addition to a long line of
award-winning children's
books that Chwast has
designed and illustrated
over the past 15 years: A
magician is bored with his
turtle—so he turns it into
a bird, a monkey, a camel,
an elephant, and then finally
back into a turtle because
Mr. Merlin realizes that he
was better off with the turtle
to begin with. All of this is
accomplished with the aid
of die-cut flaps.
Writer/Designer/Illustrator,
Seymour Chwast.

below
Mascot-like identity for
The Brooklyn Children's
Museum, NY. The logo was
designed to help expand a
young mind about the world
of science and culture.
Representing the mission of
the museum is a whimsical
robot with a propeller beak.
It ventures out and bends
over to observe a flower
that turns into a bouquet.
Designer/Illustrator,
Seymour Chwast.

opposite page
Packaging system and design
for a mathematics program by
Addison Wesley, Menlo Park,
CA. Targeted for children
from kindergarten through
the sixth grade, Chwast's
design and illustration for
the book covers and packaging
utilize question marks, representing the theme "Quest."
Art Director/Illustrator,
Seymour Chwast; designer,
Roxanne Slimak.

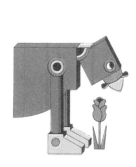
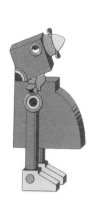

ADDISON-WESLEY

QUEST
2000

EXPLORING MATHEMATICS

GRADE 2

For Evaluation Only

ADDISON-WESLEY

QUEST
2000

EXPLORING MATHEMATICS

Literature
Libraries

ADDISON-WESLEY

QUEST
2000

EXPLORING MATHEMATICS

For Evaluation Only

The Teacher's Guide and Journal

The Professional Handbook

Grade 2

Teacher
Support File

Assessment Masters
Activity Masters
Family Masters
And More...

Math Workouts

Problem
of the Week

Transparencies

Poster
Package (K-2)

ADDISON-WESLEY

QUEST
2000

EXPLORING MATHEMATICS

GRADE 2

ADDISON-WESLEY

QUEST
2000

EXPLORING MATHEMATICS

TEACHER'S GUIDE & JOURNAL

For Evaluation Only

GRADE 2

left and bottom
An award-winning calendar that pays homage to the automobile with 14 unique illustrations of cars created in a wide range of media. When asked if any were Fords, Chwast simply said, "They're *all* Fords." Designer/Illustrator, Seymour Chwast; co-producers, Berman Printing, Mohawk Paper and The Pushpin Group.

The P Chronicles were developed as a promotion for one of the largest printing companies in the country, Ivy Hill, New York, NY. Using Pushpin's and Steven Heller's collection of books and objects, the first P Chronicle was called "Perfection," displaying "perfect" images. The second in a series, "The Package as Object," featured a collection of fine packaging from the last century. As a showcase for Ivy Hill's printing techniques and manufacturing capabilities, the background photograph of an old dry goods store adds nostalgia—a reminder of the impact packaging has had on merchandising. Note that several packages below are three-dimensional. For instance, the needle package unfolds, revealing silver-foil printing on the needles. Designers, Seymour Chwast and Greg Simpson; editor, Steven Heller.

Sagmeister Inc.

Principal: Stefan Sagmeister
Year Founded: 1993
Size of Firm: 2
Key Clients: Aerosmith, Blue, David Byrne, Dennis Hayes & Associates, HBO Studio Productions, Naked Music, RCA, Schertler Audio Transducers, Sony, Toto, Viacom, Warner Bros.

222 West 14th Street
New York, NY 10011
212 647 1789

agmeister Inc.'s West 14th Street studio spells out a kind of company mission statement—a wooden-twig sign in the studio reads: Style=Fart. "Style," says Stefan Sagmeister, "is unimportant. It's hot air. According to Webster, style is 'the making or designing in accord with a prevailing mode.' Style is what designers fall back on when they don't have a strong concept." The choice of style elements—including typefaces, illustrations and photography—is determined by the concept. Every project at Sagmeister Inc. is firmly rooted in a concept, believing that the conceptual phase is by far the most difficult, time consuming and important part of any project. Sagmeister has deliberately kept his studio small, allowing him to concentrate on a highly-select client list. "We always try to advertise and promote products we like," he says. "When you actually believe in a product, it's much easier to care about the results. There's no substitute for enthusiasm. We really love our job."

left
CD cover for Energy Records, New York, NY. Pro-Pain, a hardcore band, needed a cover that reflected the music. To illustrate the destruction of beauty, the cover was shot in a morgue of a woman who had died peacefully in her sleep. Her body was opened to determine the cause of death and then re-sewn. No retouching was done.
Designers, Stefan Sagmeister and Veronica Oh; photography, Jeffrey Silverthorne.

right
Poster for the avant-garde Jazz festival, Nickelsdorfer Konfrontationen, Austria. To advertise the festival both in and outdoors in a cost effective way, the poster was hung folded into a zig-zag in cafes and shops, while outdoors it was used flat.
Designer, Stefan Sagmeister; computer mechanical, Christian Hochmeister.

left
Incognito:
Stefan Sagmeister and
Veronica Oh.
Photography,
Ray Charles White.

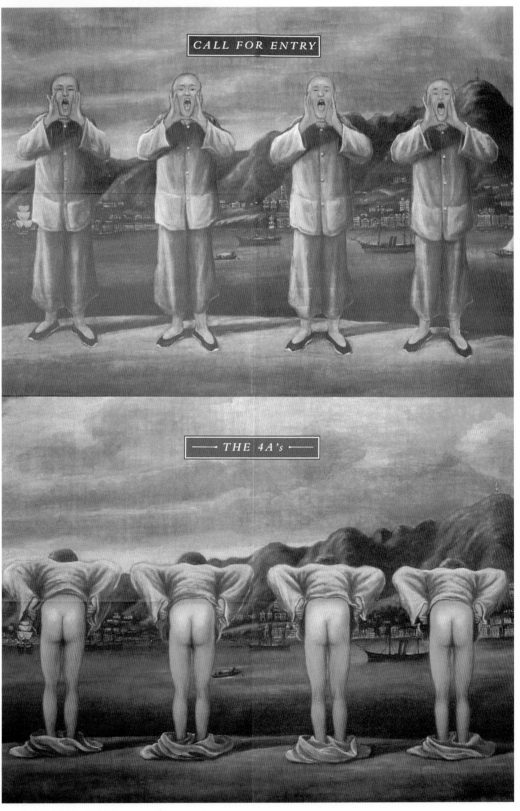

CALL FOR ENTRY

THE 4A's

left
Poster invitation of a judged competition and award show for The 4A's (The Association of Advertising Agencies), Hong Kong. The poster created a scandal in Hong Kong—it was discussed in the trade press and was shown on the cover of the *South China Morning Post*, Hong Kong's largest newspaper. Agencies threatened to take out full-page protest ads and there was talk of a competition boycott. In the end, entries were up by over 25 percent and the poster won a gold award. Designers, Stefan Sagmeister and Peter Rae; design firm, The Design Group.

below
Invitation for a gala dinner by The Gay and Lesbian Task Force, New York, NY. Designer, Stefan Sagmeister; mechanical, Tom Walker; production, Keira Alexander; creative director, Tibor Kalman; design firm, M&Co.

below
CD cover for a compilation of Portuguese influenced African music, for David Byrne/Luaka Bop, New York, NY. A hole was drilled through the entire booklet, which unified all the different photographs, illustrations, lyrics and artists. Designers, Stefan Sagmeister and Veronica Oh; photography, Tom Schierlitz.

right
CD Rom packaging for Studio SGP, New York, NY. The cover was made "interactive" for the company's multimedia demonstration disc. The logo appears in the mirror foil by rolling the cover up and sticking it into the hole of the CD. Designers, Stefan Sagmeister and Veronica Oh.

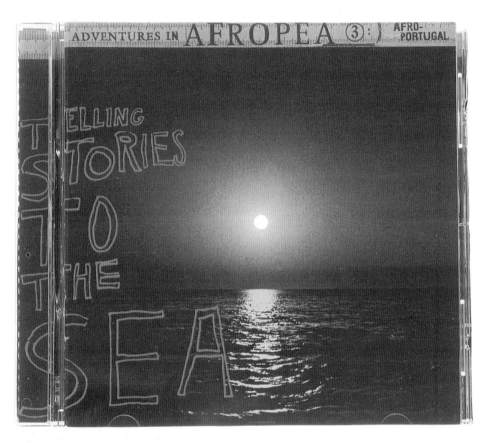

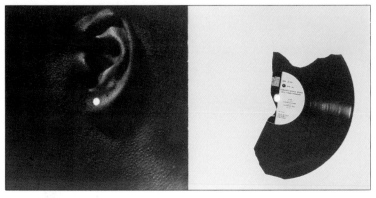

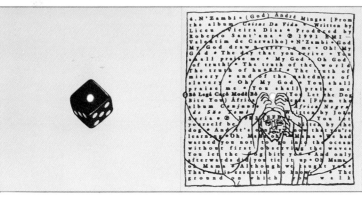

below
CD cover for the rock band, H.P. Zinker, Energy Records, New York, NY. Because the lyrics deal with angst in big city life, if you take the booklet out of the red tinted jewel case, you'll see the old man become frantic. Designers, Stefan Sagmeister and Veronica Oh; photography, Tom Schierlitz.

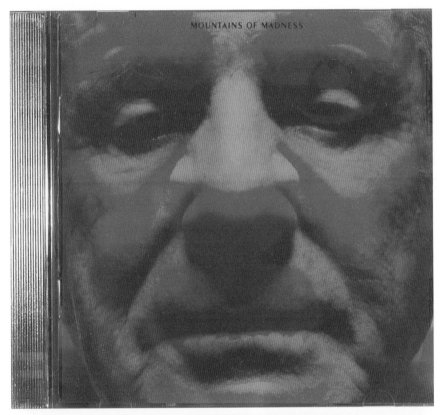

above
CD cover for Riuichi Sakamoto & YMO, a Japanese techno-band, Toshiba/EMI, Tokyo. There are 10 different covers for the consumer to choose. Each cover contains a coded message by American artist, Jenny Holzer. The message is readable only in the plastic jewel case. Designer, Stefan Sagmeister; computer mechanical, Eric Zim; creative director, Tibor Kalman; design firm, M&Co.

   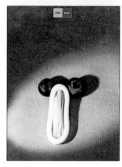  

Identity and advertising for Blue, a fashion retailer in Austria. To establish Blue as a main outlet for young fashion, a campaign was needed that couldn't be confused with any competitor's ads. "The budget was so tiny, we couldn't afford any models," says Sagmeister. "Hence the bag idea with friends sitting in." Designer, Stefan Sagmeister; photography, Tom Schierlitz; computer illustration, Kamil Vojnar; painted background, Judith Eisler.

below
Self promotional postcard. The card folds into a real working sundial. The angle can be adjusted so that it shows the correct time in most American cities. Designer, Stefan Sagmeister; computer mechanical, Veronica Oh.

below right
Stationary for Naked Music, New York, NY. "You can't get more naked than naked to the bone." Designer, Stefan Sagmeister, Veronica Oh; photography, Tom Schierlitz.

right
Identity for DHA [USA], New York, NY, a young consulting firm. Instead of a logo, all addresses and phone numbers were incorporated into the photography. The hand on the business card represents the client's hand. Designer, Stefan Sagmeister; photography, Tom Schierlitz.

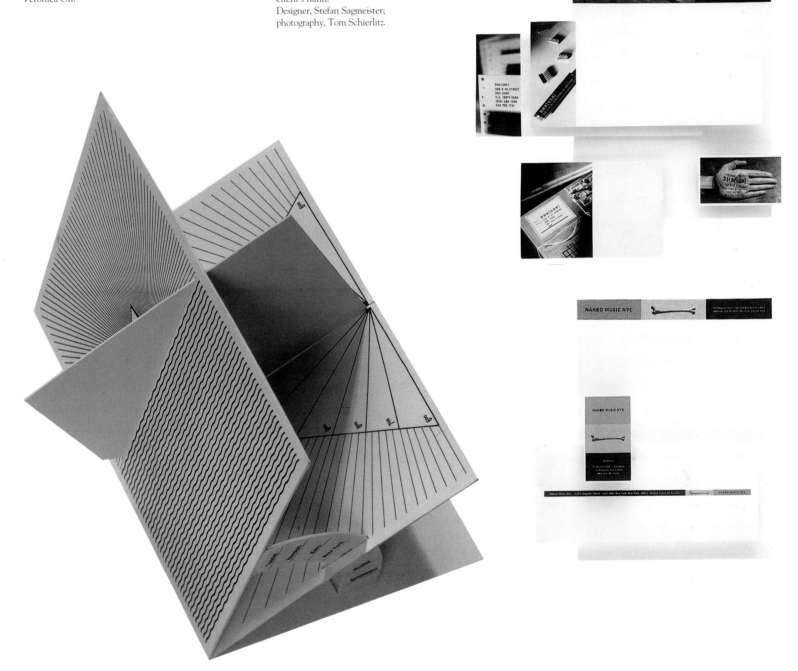

right
Self promotional postcard. The card folds into a functioning record player. The cardboard serves as a loudspeaker. Designer, Stefan Sagmeister.

Siegel & Gale

Principals:
Alan M. Siegel, Chairman;
Ken Morris, President;
Scott Lerman, EVP,
Managing Director;
Kenneth Cooke, EVP,
Creative Director;
Larry Oakner, EVP,
Creative Director;
Cheryl Heller, EVP,
Creative Director
Year Founded: 1970
Size of Firm: 150 U.S.;
200 Worldwide

Key Clients: AT&T,
American Express,
Caterpillar, Chubb, EDS,
Netscape, Harley-Davidson,
Kodak, Nations Bank,
Novartis, 3M,
360° Communications.

10 Rockefeller Plaza
New York, NY 10020
212 707 4000
www.siegelgale.com

S iegel & Gale recognizes the struggle its clients go through to create an impact in a competitive and growing market place. "A lot of our clients are playing global hardball, fighting to hang on to pieces of markets they used to own outright," says Alan Siegel. "Responding to that kind of challenge with only a redesigned logo or a new typeface is like putting a Band-Aid on a hemorrhage." Since the founding of Siegel & Gale in 1970, the company has cultivated its own communications philosophy, Corporate Voice™, that guides its work for clients. The term Corporate Voice describes the company's total expression—from job descriptions to the way its people answer phones. The design firm believes that corporate communications should be a reflection of a company's history, people, personality and views. Every vehicle, sign, product design, mailing label, annual report, advertising, interactive site, advertising campaign or product brochure is used as an opportunity to establish positive impressions about its client. It also can lead to brand preferences. Siegel contends that, "If a company's communications don't express who it is, what it does, and what it stands for, customers sense it immediately."

above
Identity system for National Semiconductor, Santa Clara, CA. The company repositioned itself from a silicon parts manufacturer to a provider of technologies that move and shape information. Known as a pioneer in the computer chip making industry, the company was a trailblazing enterprise that helped spur the development of Silicon Valley, CA. The hand is holding a computer chip that shows the smallest application of the system's new logo.

right
Name and wordmark for Nortel, Ontario, Canada. The identity positions the company as the global resource for designing, building and integrating *A World of Networks*.

right
Logo design for Secretaria de Turismo de Argentina, Buenos Aires. To boost the country's tourism value, S&G's London office created "Land of the Six Continents" with the image of an Andean condor, showing both Argentina's versatile geography and sophistication.

Argentina
Land of the six continents

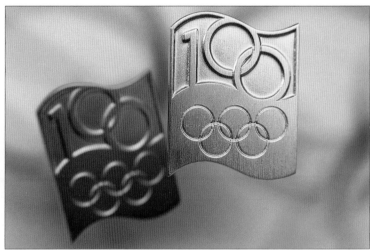

above
Cover of annual report for National Semiconductor, Santa Clara, CA. The dynamic corporate symbol conveys the company's movement, symbolizing its position within the computer chip industry.

above right
A pin to celebrate the Olympic Centennial. Reserved exclusively for the International Olympic Committee and worldwide sponsors, the logo and design program will be used to promote the spirit and enduring values that the Olympics were founded on in 1896.

New Zealand

left
Logo created for the New Zealand Trade Board, Auckland. Utilizing the silver fern—the national flower—the symbol captures the country's "fresh, unsullied" image.

above
The symbol's popularity took an unexpected turn by becoming the country's trademark. It's now used for tourism, boating, livestock, agriculture, and New Zealand's Olympic uniforms.

The New Zealand Way

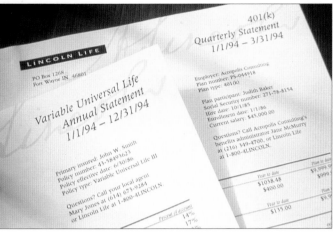

above
Simplified insurance forms save time and improve accuracy of critical information for Lincoln Life, Fort Wayne, IN.

right
Logo for Lincoln Life, utilizing Abraham Lincoln's signature. The company holds the largest collection of Lincoln memorabilia in the country. The company chairman described the old Lincoln Life identity as "the biggest unknown life insurance company in the United States."

A. Lincoln

LINCOLN LIFE

Statue of President & Mrs. Lincoln, East Park, Racine, WI.

above
Interactive screen for agent information. Part of Lincoln Life's corporate identity program uses imagery connected with the company's presidential name-sake in order to suggest "Lincoln-esque" values, such as honesty, straightforwardness and integrity, and associate them with the company.

right
Advertisement for Lincoln Life. The ad serves as a reminder of the company's values. The choice of models and setting in the photograph reinforce the company's traditional, midwestern voice while placing the statue of Lincoln and his wife in the background.

**Our basic principle for retirement planning:
no two couples are alike.**

Everyone thinks about retiring. And while we all have different plans, Lincoln Life is a life insurance company with 90 years of expertise in financial planning to help you meet your goals.

Our agents can develop a comprehensive retirement plan for you from a broad range of pension plans and individual annuities. That's the kind of personal attention which has made us a leader in pension plans and the number one issuer of individual annuities in America for three years in a row.* Honest answers, straight talk, real compassion. Those were Lincoln's values. And that's what you'll get from Lincoln Life today. And long after you've retired.

A. Lincoln

LINCOLN LIFE

*Best's Review Nov. 1992 and 1993, Oct. 1994 for years 1991, 1992, 1993
©1994 Lincoln National Life Insurance Co. Fort Wayne, Indiana 46801*   *As seen in Newsweek, Inc., Money, Business Week, Reader's Digest and Ebony.*

Eight months after the Gulf War, we declared a cease-fire of our own.

CATERPILLAR

above
Print advertisement for Caterpillar, Peoria, IL. The ad is one of a series that shows the U.S.-based global company as a major participant in world events. The series communicates to its target audience the raw authenticity, value, and significance of the product.

below
"Voice Book," a complete identity system guide for Caterpillar. The book establishes guidelines that allow a decentralized global corporation to communicate with a large audience in a consistent way. The book helps in preparing their annual report and other Caterpillar communications worldwide. S&G also developed and conducted tutorial seminars to show employees how to make Caterpillar's voice a part of all its communications.

above
Annual report cover design for Caterpillar. The report communicates that Caterpillar is a successful leader in a highly competitive global market.

below
Logo for The Birmingham Marketing Partnership, Birmingham, U.K. The logo's style differentiates it from other "old-world" European cities to convey a modern image.

right
Identity, logomark, name and type for 360°. When Sprint Cellular spun off from its parent last year it needed a way to quickly position and communicate its new identity. The name—combined with the nontraditional green signature color and distinctive corporate symbol—launched 360° into the marketplace.

above
"Think Globally and Act Locally," logo design for Bates Worldwide, New York, NY, a multinational advertising agency. The logo links different Bates Worldwide organizations without imposing upon its individual identities.

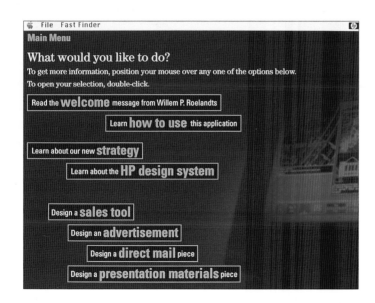

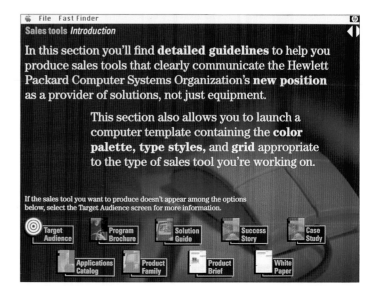

left
Corporate logo identity for Cunard, New York, NY. Without sacrificing Cunard's character, customer recognition and its 155 year-old history, the laurel wreath that surrounded and dominated the Cunard name was removed and the classic Cunard lion, the company's crest, was simplified and made more prominent. The logotype was refined and a tricolor stripe added to create a branding system for the entire fleet.

right
Bathrobe on the *Queen Elizabeth 2*, Cunard.
far right
Invitation for *Queen Elizabeth 2*, Cunard.

---

left and opposite page
Interactive software for Hewlett Packard Computer Systems, Cupertino, CA. The software guides writers and designers to carry forward the look, message and tone of voice of an innovative Hewlett Packard ad campaign. The system was designed to share common elements with a new campaign developed by the company's advertising agency, Saatchi Pacific. Developed for collateral applications, the system is intended for anyone who works on Hewlett Packard materials, in-house or through an outside supplier.

above
MTA, New York City's Metropolitan Transit Authorities introduction to the first automatic fare payment card linking all the transit services the agency operates. MTA needed a communications system that informed New Yorkers about the scope of the agency's operations before they introduced the MetroCard program in 1994. The program was recognized by the American Institute of Graphic Arts, and Industrial Designers Society of America.

Slatoff + Cohen Partners Inc.

Principals: David Slatoff, Tamar Cohen
Year Founded: 1992
Size of Firm: 4
Key Clients:
Coach Leatherware, 4AD Records, HarperCollins, Lincoln Center Theaters, Marvel Entertainment, Metropolitan Transporation Authority, MTV Networks, Nickelodeon, Sony Corporation of America, The Cartoon Network, Gap, The Monet Group. Warner Bros. Studio Stores.

17 West 20 Street
New York, NY 10011
212 243 8019

Slatoff + Cohen Partners Inc. is a firm whose fresh, eclectic work is grounded in the classic traditions of 20th-century graphic design. David Slatoff and Tamar Cohen learned the rigorous Modernist tenets of clarity and form at established New York design firms, graduating to the freer, more experimental studio, Doublespace. There they met and struck up a collaborative relationship that eventually became the foundation of their own company. During the three years since Slatoff + Cohen's inception, the firm has established a broad roster of clients. From informational design to packaging, their work exhibits a strong sense of color, contemporary typography, and a resourceful flair for concise metaphors and illustrative solutions. The partners find inspiration in the sublime and banal, traveling frequently to enrich their visual vocabularies and collecting printed ephemera from around the world. The result is a blend of clear and evocative messages with a unique and surprising style of delivery.

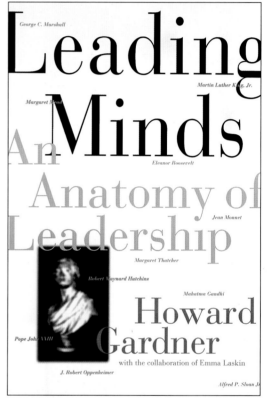

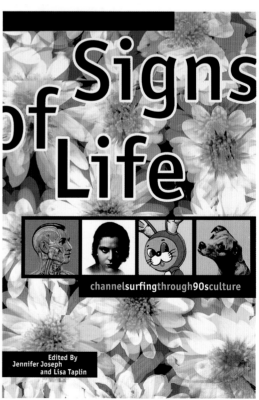

top right
Jacket design for Basic Books, a division of HarperCollins, New York, NY.

right
Jacket design for a collection of stories, poetry and comics for manic d press, San Francisco, CA.

left
Logotype design and promotional piece for photographer Joshua McHugh, New York, NY.

left
Tamar Cohen
and David Slatoff.
Photography,
Ray Charles White.

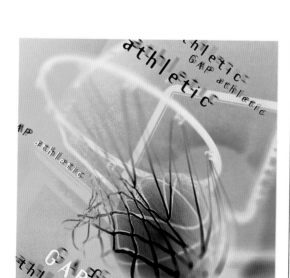

above and above left
Press kit and logotype for
Electrokinetics, New York,
NY. The company special-
izes in electro-mechanical
design and engineering.
Photography, Joshua
McHugh.

left
Apparel graphics applied to
mens and boys shirts for the
Gap, New York, NY.

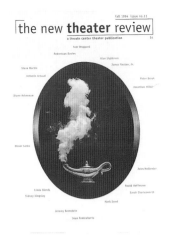

opposite page
Broadcast design for Nickelodeon, New York, NY. A series of highly re-watchable bumpers and menus were created that would project an international feel, contain constant network identification, and a stable video window to show specific footage. Nickelodeon Creative Directors, Scott Webb and Steve Thomas; animation, Jeff Sargeant.

left and below
A quarterly publication for Lincoln Center Theater, New York, NY. It includes essays, interviews, play excerpts, poetry and art. Cover artwork, Sarah Charlesworth, Weegee, Shinro Ohtake and Rudy Burckhardt. Interior art-work, Pierre et Gilles.

below
Identity for the photographer, Frank W. Ockenfels 3, New York, NY. The system included the logotype, stationery and promotional cards.

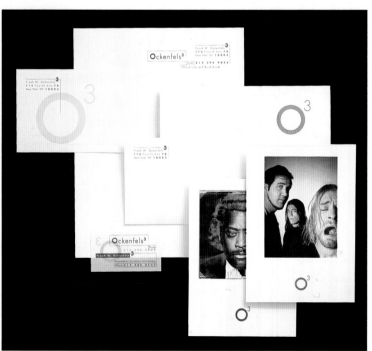

Ockenfels³

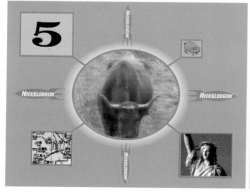

left
Jacket design for Alfred A.
Knopf, New York, NY. The
composite photograph on
the back cover was woven
together by hand.
Black and white photography, Mark Hill.

below
Jacket design for St. Martin's
Press, New York, NY.
Photography, Tom Collicott.

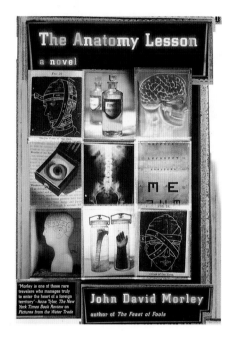

right
A catalog cover for Ex
Libris, a bookstore that
specializes in rare 20th
Century avant garde art
books, New York, NY.

below
Brush and cosmetic accessory packaging for Revlon,
produced by Phillips
Industries, Long Island
City, New York. The project was a collaboration
with Handler, the industrial design firm who created
the brushes.
Principal, Laura Handler;
head designer, Amanda
Honig Magalhaes.

below
Brochures for the
Metropolitan Transportation
Authority Card Company,
which announces the arrival
of the MetroCard on buses
and subways in New York.

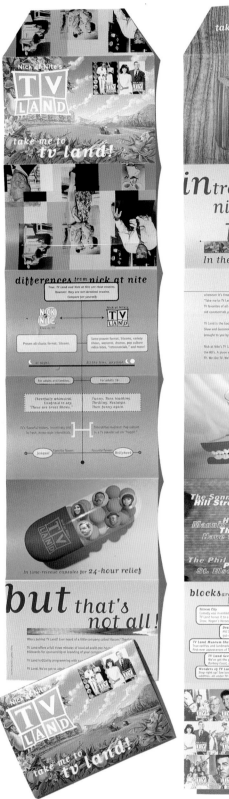

left
Calendar for 4AD records,
London. The non-func-
tional wall calendar is based
on the theme of anatomy.
This project was designed
in collaboration with
Vaughan Oliver of V23.

below left
Calendar based on the idea
of a numbered environ-
ment, for V23, London.

left
A promotional piece
introducing Nick at Nite's
new television network,
"TV Land." Inspired by the
concept, "Take me to TV
Land," the piece was
designed in the form of an
unfolding postcard booklet.
On the last panel of the

booklet is a set of remov-
able self-adhesive "stamps"
highlighting the network's
programming.
Cover illustration, George
Bates; dental still life
photography, Christopher
Gallo; 3-D capsule
illustration, Joe Fernandez.

Slover [AND] Company

Principal: Susan Slover
Year Founded: 1984
Size of Firm: 12
Key Clients: Bergdorf-
Goodman, Burlington
Industries, Chronical
Books: Giftwork Division,
Coach Leathergoods,
Donghia Furniture/Textiles,
Echo Design Group,
FilaSport, Hoechst
Celanese, L'Oreal,
New York Botanical
Gardens, Sara Lee
Intimates: Bali Division.

584 Broadway
Suite 903
New York, NY 10012

'Slover [AND] Company's principal Susan Slover says, in a faint southern drawl, that she likes to "mix things up." Whether a client is corporate or retail, local or global, "We like to do things differently," she says. "Of course, our design has to solve our client's business problems, but lately the biggest problem may be that it's all starting to look alike out there." Not so with Slover designs. The firm created the distinctive packaging for Takashimaya and redefined the shape of the shopping bag; developed corporate giant Sara Lee's language for the Bali Intimate's "un-d's" and created the successfully illustrated, mass market "Everygal." Slover notes that as soon as clients bring the firm into their business process, she pulls them into the firm's creative process. "We get in the car, put the top down, and head hard left to what everyone else seems to think is right. When we break ninety-miles an hour, the ideas just can't hold themselves back."

A distinctly different bag and box program for Takashimaya, New York, NY. The retailer's North American flagship store's new program is architectural, asymmetrical, and engineered to fold flat for economical shipping and storage.

left
An eight-part advertising campaign for Saks Fifth Avenue, New York, NY, ran in cities where the stores had undergone massive renovation. The full-page ads ran consecutively, integrated with type that delivered "impulse" messages. The photography—a visual metaphor—is not intended to sell Saks product, but rather the Saks persona. The message: Saks Fifth Avenue, now like never before.

below left
Proprietary product design that uses simple but strong typographic patterns. A storewide identity for over 200 private label products was created, constructed from the Sak's logo. Product categories include food, cosmetics, accessories and stationery. The proprietary patterns are generally reproduced in two colors, making the program both powerful and economical.

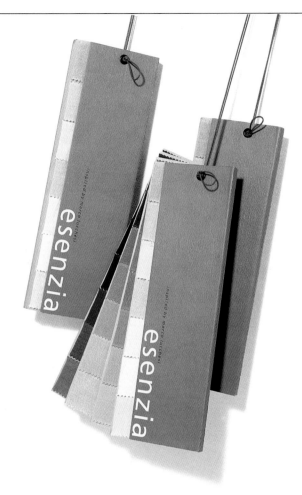

Clockwise from top
Waterfall fabric selectors; tools for the trade; market invitation using macro-photography by Craig Cutler; showroom environment.

Identity system for Burlington Industries, New York, NY. When America's largest mass manufacturer of fashion textiles wanted to embrace the luxury market, it needed a completely different product and selling approach. Slover [AND] Company named the collection "esenzia" and developed selling tools and an environment that visually—and viscerally—reinforced the essential character of the collection. The result was a soft selling approach that produced cold, hard sales in a flat-end market.

Touch Kits—hand-sewn from textured papers and closed with a button and leather thong—were given to fashion editors and designers to reinforce the essential selling message.

Brochure for The Wicker
Collection, Donghia
Furniture/ Textiles, New
York, NY. Wall-to-wall
photographic textures help
the reader "feel" the handmade nature of the furniture.
The brochure is loop-
stitched and printed in
three languages for international markets.

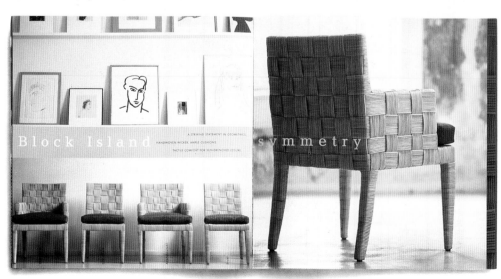

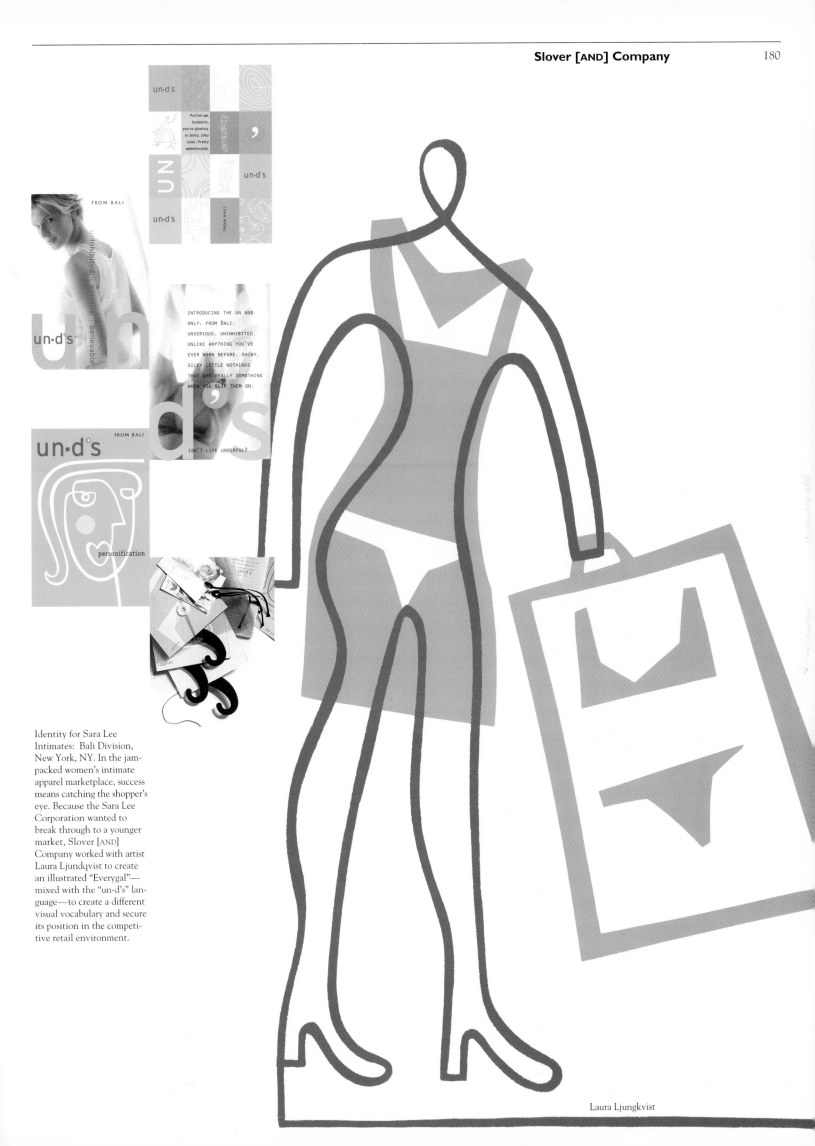

un·d's

Put 'em un.
Suddenly,
you're glowing.
In shiny, silky
color. Pretty
unbelievable.

un·d's

UN

un·d's

FROM BALI

FROM BALI

uninhibited un·serious un·believable

un·d's

INTRODUCING THE UN AND
ONLY. FROM BALI.
UNSERIOUS. UNINHIBITED.
UNLIKE ANYTHING YOU'VE
EVER WORN BEFORE. SHINY,
SILKY LITTLE NOTHINGS
THAT ARE REALLY SOMETHING
WHEN YOU SLIP THEM ON.

ISN'T LIFE UNDERFUL?

FROM BALI

un·d's

personification

Identity for Sara Lee
Intimates: Bali Division,
New York, NY. In the jam-
packed women's intimate
apparel marketplace, success
means catching the shopper's
eye. Because the Sara Lee
Corporation wanted to
break through to a younger
market, Slover [AND]
Company worked with artist
Laura Ljundqvist to create
an illustrated "Everygal"—
mixed with the "un-d's" language—to create a different
visual vocabulary and secure
its position in the competitive retail environment.

Laura Ljungkvist

GAS
AUTO
TAXI
EPAIRS
OPEN
24 HOURS
REPAIRS
24
HRS.
OPEN
REPAIRS
24

Smart Design

Principals:
Thomas Dair, Stephen
Russak, Davin Stowell,
Tamara Thomsen,
Tucker Viemeister.
Year Founded: 1979
Size of Firm: 24
Key Clients: Alpine
Electronics, Apple
Computer, Aris Isotoner,
AT&T, Corning,
Cuisinarts, Daewoo,
General Housewares,
Johnson & Johnson,
Kepner-Tregoe, Levi
Strauss & Co., Timex.

137 Varick Street
New York, NY 10013
212 807 8150

Smart Design's mission is simple: to produce smart design for fun and profit. Since 1979, consumer product companies have relied upon Smart Design to solve users' needs—both physical and emotional. "All our work has to fit the mind, as well as the body," says Tucker Viemeister. "Psychonomics is as important as ergonomics when developing a smart design." Smart uses design to connect with the consumer and build a long-lasting relationship, not just a product. According to Tam Thomsen, "A lot of people don't know what they like until they see it. So we listen for unspoken desires in the marketplace, and turn it into consumer demand. For us that's fun...for the client that's profit."

left, above and opposite page
Wacky watches and packaging for Timex, Middlebury, CT. The watches were designed with Nicholas Graham under the "Joe Boxer" license. Designers, Debbie Hahn, Paul Hamburger, Stephanie Kim and Tucker Viemeister.

above
Reach WonderGrip Kids Toothbrush for Johnson & Johnson, Skillman, NJ. Research and psychonomic design of a toothbrush. It's a brush that children want to use and can easily hold onto. Industrial Design and Research, Tom Dair, Dan Formosa, Davin Stowell and Tam Thomsen.

left
Left to right, top row:
Jurgen Parlowski, Stephen
Russak, Jarrod Linton,
Tom Dair, Greg Littleton,
Scott Bolden, Edwin Chan,
Tam Thomsen; bottom row:
Evelyn Teploff, Debbie
Hahn, Carly White,
Paul Hamburger, Tracy
McKenna, Scott Henderson,
Stephanie Kim, Vanessa
Sica, Mari Ando, Cathy
Cervenka, Tucker Viemeister,
Davin Stowell.

below
Centennial celebration
logo, lecture series posters
and announcements for the
University of Nebraska
School of Architecture,
Lincoln, NE.
Designers, Debbie Hahn,
Paul Hamburger and
Tam Thomsen.

right
*Healthy Women, Healthy
Mothers*, an illustrated guide
for African women and
health care workers for
Family Care International,
New York, NY.
Designers, Debbie Hahn,
Evelyn Teploff and
Tam Thomsen.

above
Marketing brochure for
Kepner-Tregoe, Princeton,
NJ. One of the world's largest
training and consulting firms,
the brochure uses friendly,
even humorous illustrations
to explain sophisticated services and products.
Designer, Paul Hamburger;
illustrator, James Yang.

left and opposite page bottom
Identity and announcements,
and course-offering catalogs
for Urban Glass, a glass
workshop in Brooklyn, NY.
Designers, Evelyn Teploff
and Tucker Viemeister.

left
Identity, training manuals and membership directories for the Association of Junior Leagues International, New York, NY.
Designers, Stephanie Kim, Evelyn Teploff and Tam Thomsen.

below
Training manuals and workbooks for Kepner-Tregoe, Princeton, NJ. The company provides a variety of training and consulting services to some of the largest corporations in the world. This specific product was designed at a ninth-grade reading level for shop floor employees. Icons and illustrations, including comic book style graphics, were used to make the materials more interesting and easy to understand.
Designers, Dan Formosa, Rie Norregaard, Davin Stowell and Stacy Walsh.

left
Serengeti sunglasses for
Corning Inc., Corning, NY.
High-end, high-tech, high-
fashion sun eyewear. Logo,
identity, packaging, consumer
brochures, trade catalogs and
point-of-purchase displays
were part of the program.
Designers, Debbie Hahn,
Stephanie Kim, Rie
Norregaard and Davin
Stowell; industrial designers,
Tom Dair, Jurgen Parlowski,
David Peschel, Vanessa
Sica, Davin Stowell and
Tucker Viemeister.

right/below
An information-rich retail
environment for Dockers
Authentics shop-in-shop for
Levi Strauss & Co., San
Francisco, CA. The pants are
arranged on shelves and in
drawers so customers can find
their size quickly and easily.
Designer, Michael Sonato;
industrial designers, Tucker
Viemeister; architecture,
Henry Meyerberg; strategy,
David Hales.

below and opposite page bottom
Kitchen gadgets and pack-
aging for Oxo International,
General Housewares Corp.,
Terre Haute, IN. The prod-
uct's handle makes the
utensils easy to use. Product
name, logo, and identity,
one for department stores
(GoodGrips), and one for
mass market (Prima).
Designers, Stephanie Kim,
Rie Norregaard, Davin
Stowell and Evelyn Teploff;
industrial designers,
Stephan Allendorf,
Mari Ando, Scott Bolden,
Jurgen Parlowski, Stephen
Russak, Davin Stowell and
Tucker Viemeister.

opposite page/left
Identity and packaging of
Home Phone, for Cicena,
New York, NY. The phone
is comfortable, economical
and easy-to-use.
Designer, Evelyn Teploff;
industrial designers, Tucker
Viemeister and Stuart Lee.

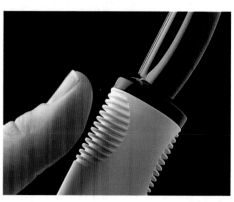

below right
Umbrella design, brand identity and packaging for Aris Isotoner, New York, NY. The new WonderGrip umbrella features an easy-to-hold soft handle. The packaging was designed to make sure the consumer could feel the handle. Designers, Evelyn Teploff, Stephanie Kim and Tam Thomsen; industrial designers, Mari Ando, Jarrod Linton and Davin Stowell.

right
Oral contraceptive trade packaging and identity for Berlex Laboratories, Wayne, NJ. Designers, Evelyn Teploff and Tam Thomsen.

Studio Morris

Principals: Jeffrey Morris,
Patricia Kovic
Year Founded: 1988
Size of Firm: 12
Key Clients: Reuters,
Morgan Stanley, Hot Sox,
JMLynne, AIM 21.

55 Vandam Street
Suite 901
New York, NY 10013
212 366 0401

Studio Morris provides the best of both worlds—the personal service and fresh ideas of a small design firm combined with the depth of design and marketing expertise of larger companies. Specializing in integrated communication programs, the firm uses a holistic approach to solve strategic and communication problems. Principals Jeffrey Morris and Patricia Kovic believe these programs are suitable to individual brands and corporations alike. The firm's design philosophy combines Kovic's intuitive working style and Morris' rational approach. Both Morris and Kovic are emphatic in their belief that design is not simply decoration, but a process for solving problems and creating opportunity. This belief accounts for the firm's diversity in clientele—ranging from fashion and contract furnishing to new media and finance. Studio Morris has won numerous design awards, and both principals are visiting professors in the Graduate Design program at Pratt Institute.

Shown: *Fresco/Mimosa Series Commercial Vinyl Wallcovering*
Design: *Patty Madden*
For more information: 800 645 5044

above right
Integrated communications program for JMLynne. To re-position the company to compete with other high-end contract wallcovering companies, and to focus on the company's core strengths, the program implemented a tag line, corporate identity, advertising wall covering books and trade show booths. Designers, Jeffrey Morris and Kaoru Sato; photography, Doug Rosa; copywriter, Lisa Friedman.

right
Trademark and wall covering book design for Blumenthal Inc. to increase awareness and improve presentation of the product, the design positioned the company as a leading wall covering supplier. The design of the books' structure also saved the company 40 percent on manufacturing costs. Designer, Jeffrey Morris; marketing consultant, Georgina Walker.

left
Jeffrey Morris.
Photography,
Ray Charles White.

below
Aalto brochure for
International Contract
Furnishings. Created to target consumers rather than
the traditional architect
and designer market, the
existing photography was
combined with hip lifestyle
photography. The rounded
edges of the brochure
reflect the rounded edges of
the furniture.

Designers, Jeffrey Morris
and Patricia Kovic; stock
photography, Photonica;
copywriter, Lisa Friedman.

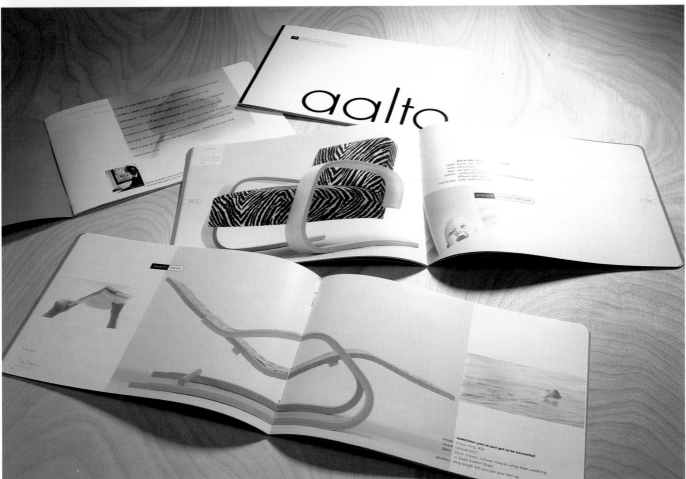

far right
Shopping bags for Unika
Vaev. Printed on translucent,
recyclable plastic, the bag
helped to attract visitors to
the company's showroom
during "Neocon," an indus-
try-wide show in Chicago.
Designers, Jeffrey Morris,
Patricia Kovic and
Kaoru Sato.

right
Catalog sheets for
International Contract
Furnishings. The sheets were
the first implementation of
a marketing communications
system. A totally transparent
design solution allows the
furniture to be the hero. Most
of the furniture is in the
MOMA Design collection.
Designers, Jeffrey Morris,
Patricia Kovic and
Kaoru Sato; photography,
Abby Sadin.

left
Campaign to promote
Artwalk for the Coalition
for the Homeless, a day
where artists in New York
open their studios to walking tours. Posters, brochures
and advertising explain the
tours. A gritty, "from the
streets," logo was placed over
a diffused rose. The stark
contrast between the juxtaposed images communicates
its mission.
Designers, Jeffrey Morris
and Kaoru Sato.

left
Integrated communica-
tions program for Hot Sox
Hosiery. This five-year
program established a
distinctive "voice" and
positioning for the com-
pany—during which
time the company's rev-
enue doubled. The pro-
gram comprised of a logo,
identity system, advertising, packaging, point-of-
purchase displays and marketing communications.
Designer, Jeffrey Morris;
photography,
Jaime Phillips.

below
Name development,
brand identity and word-
mark for Double Take,
a franchise of consignment
boutiques. The challenge
was to take the concept
of a second-hand clothing
store and make it upscale,
fashionable and franchis-
able. Hang tags were sug-
gested as a way of unifying
the merchandise in a store
that only carries one of
everything.
Designers, Jeffrey Morris
and Patricia Kovic.

right
Hosiery package for Ralph
Lauren. The project was
designed to be sold in a
department store environ-
ment where it would be
competing with other
brands, instead of just in
the Ralph Lauren stores.
Designer, Jeffrey Morris.

right
Point-of-purchase display
for Hot Sox. The display
relates to the packaging, as
does the advertising and all
communication materials.
Designer, Jeffrey Morris.

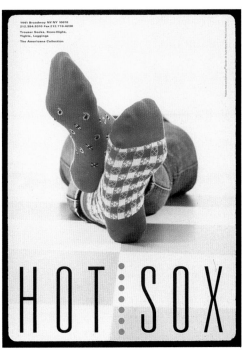

above
"Feet" ad, the first advertisement in the trade campaign showing the new
products that the company
was designing.
Designer, Jeffrey Morris;
photography, Lizzie Himmel.

left
Bus shelter poster for Hot
Sox. The image grabs
immediate attention as well
as advertises that Hot Sox
makes animal patterned
legwear.
Designer, Jeffrey Morris;
photography, Lizzie Himmel.

right
Service mark and brochure
for an on-line triage service,
Oxford Health Insurance.
The objective was to create
an identity and communi-
cate to doctors how the
program works. The triangle
logo design symbolizes the
connection between Oxford,
doctors and patients.
Designers, Jeffrey Morris,
Kaoru Sato and Banu Berker;
photography, Bard Martin.

In the Business of Risk.

You Need to Know.

Reuters Insurance Information
Profit from Intelligence.

Plans for an international trade center are announced:
Twin commercial towers and a new tunnel will be built
in an expanding Southeast Asian capital.

The **prospects** for new business are enormous—
there will be construction and fire risk for the
project; liability insurance for the architects and
construction companies—and an insurance policy
for the completed structures.

To turn a cold lead into a solid opportunity,
the enterprising insurance Broker needs up-to-date,
full reports on the project.

Reuters Insurance Information delivers.

Use Reuters Insurance Information to identify opportunities—in every
part of the world. Develop new products. Penetrate new markets.
Expand your market share.

You can analyze your key market sectors—in the countries you select.
Monitor the top players. Follow the market issues. Single out new-product trends.
With Reuters Insurance Information as your new-business partner.

The *Essential*
New-Business Tool

*"In today's business climate, where information is important,
the Reuters Insurance Briefing is a unique service. There is no
other place you can get information quickly and precisely
without plowing through hardcopy. Insurance executives who
wish to get a global view of the insurance industry are missing
out if they do not have the Insurance Briefing."*

Simon Brett
Chief Executive Officer
Curlingford Insurance
Hong Kong

above
Communications kit for
Reuters Insurance Briefing,
an on-line business information service for the insurance
industry. Specific, real-life
examples were used showing
the kinds of information
available with the services,
creating a sense of immediacy
and understanding.
Designers, Jeffrey Morris
and Kaoru Sato; writer,
Lisa Friedman.

right
Corporate identity for the
Republic New York
Corporation, one of the
largest financial services
corporations in the world.
To unify global branding of
all subsidiaries and establish
a cohesive identity system,
the solution could not be
flashy. "Understatement"
was key to communicating
the conservative and stable
corporate culture.
Designers, Jeffrey Morris,
Diane Davidson and
Kaoru Sato.

Integrated communications program for Reuters Business Briefing. The on-line service was "branded" and positioned vis-a-vis the competition, which are primarily software companies. The imagery is metaphoric and ethereal, a unique touch for these business-to-business communications. Designers, Jeffrey Morris, Kaoru Sato and Banu Berker; writer, David Konigsberg.

The product kit consists of various pieces. The image of the hand touching water is for the "Server" version of the product, used to target Managers of Information Services. The back of the pieces used a series of collages, which were also used as an 8-by-10-foot trade show wall.

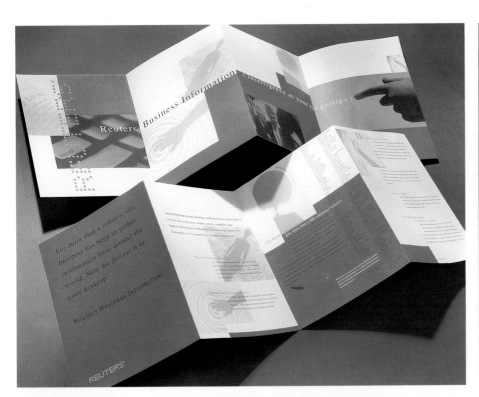

For more than a century, our primary business has been to gather intelligence from around the world.

Now we deliver it to your desktop.

No matter what your role in business, you need fast, accurate, reliable information. About your industry. About your customers. About your competitors. About the world. Reuters Business Briefing and Reuters Business Alert deliver that intelligence around the clock. For the individual or for the group. On line 24 hours a day.

Call 1.800.383.6335

Reuters, Reuter and the dotted logo are registered trademarks of Reuters Limited in more than 25 countries.

REUTERS
Reuters Business Information
(Intelligence at Your Fingertips)

Two Twelve Group

Principals: David Gibson,
Ann Harakawa,
Julie Marable
Year Founded: 1980
Size of Firm: 25
Key Clients:
Carnegie Institute, Chicago
Park District, Massachusetts
General Hospital, New York
City Housing Authority,
T. Rowe Price, Steelcase,
Times Square Business
Improvement District,
U.S. Bureau of the Census,
Walt Disney Imagineering.

596 Broadway
Suite 1212
New York, NY 10012-3233
212 925 6885
www.twotwelve.com

Two Twelve provides public access to places, products and ideas for large, broad-based audiences. The firm specializes in helping government, corporate and institutional clients change to a customer-focused orientation. "Our clients need more effective tools to communicate," says David Gibson, Two Twelve's founding principal, "and we are increasingly finding that to present a complete information program requires a combination of media." Three teams at Two Twelve bring focused expertise to these disciplines: print communications, environmental graphics and interactive media. Underlying all of Two Twelve's work is a humanistic approach to design, which reflects the personalities of its principals. They share a passion for the field and a common belief that aesthetics should grow out of end use, rather than letting style drive design. In Two Twelve's design solutions, sequence and navigation come first, typography is crisp and communicative; clarity and coherence are distinctive to the work. It is graphic design that motivates and empowers people.

above
Series of brochures for the Times Square Business Improvement District, New York, NY. The communications program presents the district as an exciting, viable and safe place to visit and conduct business. It includes a business-to-business marketing brochure, visitor, hotel and restaurant guides, and a fact guide about the BID. Art Director, Julie Marable; designers, Michael Dabbs, Susan Carabetta and John Paolini.

right
Logo for People With Aids Coalition New York. PWACNY is a community-based information and support organization for people with AIDS and HIV. The talking bubble logo expresses—in a lighthearted way—the dialogue that is at the heart of the organization. A sticker of the logo can be put in the most provocative places.
Art Director, David Gibson; designer, David Reinfurt.

left
From left: Julie Marable,
David Gibson and
Ann Harakawa.
Photography,
Ray Charles White.

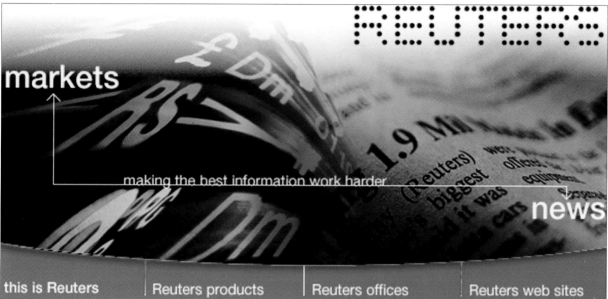

this is Reuters · Reuters products · Reuters offices · Reuters web sites

Website for Reuters, the largest wholesaler of news and information. Three websites were designed and developed: corporate, business and consumer. Work included design of the home page screens, the user interface design and the creation of the underlying navigational system for the sites. Designer, David Reinfurt.

left and below
Home page and text pages for the the Reuter's corporate site.

left
Reuter's *Newsmachine* is a consumer site. An icon called "My News" allows users to identify their areas of interest and pre-select news.

Architectural graphics for the new Federal Courthouse building at Foley Square, New York, NY. Featuring a classic, understated design, the building's circulation patterns accommodate three completely non-intersecting paths for the public, judges and staff, and prisoners. The signage meets stringent security, building code and ADA regulations.
Art Directors, David Gibson and Ann Harakawa; designer, Ben Goodman; project manager, Andy Simons.

right and below
A modular system for room identification plaques allows for variations within a well-defined framework. All plaques feature a combination of fixed room number panels and changeable components including the name plate, the classical header, and a sloped dimensional Braille panel.

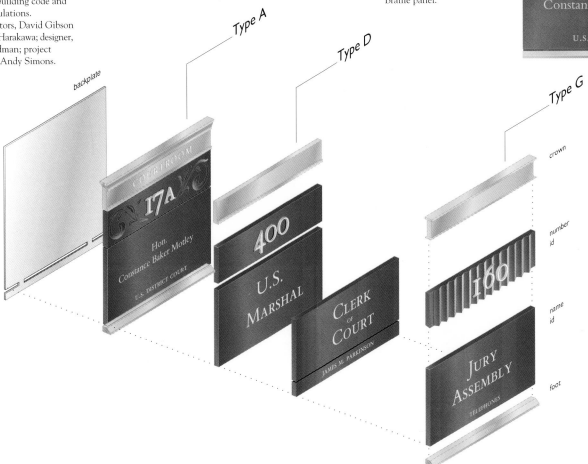

backplate

Type A

Type D

Type G

crown

number id

name id

foot

below
The all-caps display of the
Bembo typeface was particularly appropriate for the
carved building identification on the entrance's
stonework.

below
The graphic design team
looked for imagery without
political or religious over-
tones. This elegant floral
motif was used as a pattern
on courtroom signage.

opposite page and above
The General Services
Administration, as well as
the judges' committee, felt
strongly that the design of
the building should convey
dignity, classicism and a sense
of restraint and timelessness.

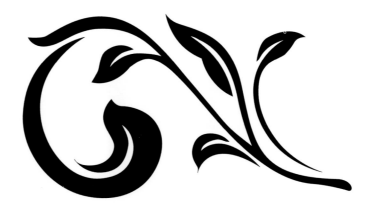

right
To introduce its Variable
Annuities retirement prod-
uct, the investment firm
T. Rowe Price needed a
direct marketing package.
The kit includes a "Variable
Annuity Analyzer" disk with
custom software as well as
print collateral.
Print Art Director, Julie
Marable, print designer,
Ellen Conant; interactive
design director, David Peters;
editorial director, Deborah
Kaufman; production
designer, Diana Zantopp.

right
Using the Analyzer disk,
investors can compare
investing in a variable
annuity versus mutual
funds, and personalize the
comparison based on age,
amount invested, projected
return, and other factors.
This software is the first
instance of the SEC
approving a computerized
marketing tool that pro-
vides scenarios of both the
accrual of invested funds
as well as their distribution.

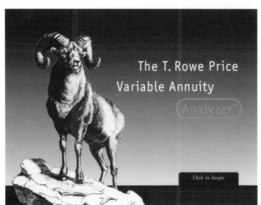

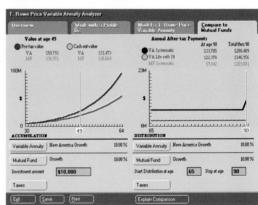

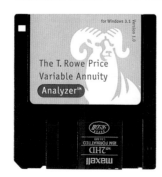

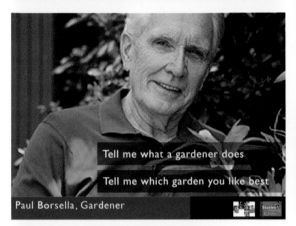

A unified and updated graphic identity was applied to publications, visitor guides, signage and interactive exhibits for the New York Botanical Garden, located in the Bronx. It is one of America's premiere public gardens and research centers. Art directors, David Gibson and Julie Marable; designer, Jennifer Wagner; interactive designer, David Peters; environmental graphics, Gibson and Nicholas Grohe.

above
Special events brochures, the visitor guides and the annual report share a common visual theme and graphic approach.

Interactive video screens (*top*) acknowledge the international, multi-lingual nature of visitors; guests can choose from several languages to be guided by "real people" stories of one, two and four-hour, as well as all-day visits. An appropriately decorative temporary barrier (*above*) provides information and site decoration during the renovation of the Enid Haupt Conservatory. The signage and wayfinding system (*right and left*) incorporates colors and typefaces developed in the identity program.

Victore Design Works

Principal: James Victore
Year Founded: 1986
Size of Firm: 2
Key Clients: Amnesty
International, USA; Carol
Publishing Group,
Coalition for the Homeless,
Elektra Entertainment,
Farrar, Straus and Giroux;
Grove/Atlantic, NAACP,
National Association for
the Advancement of
Colored People; New York
Times, The Shakespeare
Project, Viacom, Warner
Classics International.

64 Grand Street
Second Floor
New York, NY 10013
212 925 6862

Victore Design Works is dedicated to creating beautiful and striking images for a diverse group of clients. Distinguished by strong graphic ideas, visual wit and using bold, often aggressive imagery, James Victore's work has quickly attracted international attention—his poster depicting the horror of racism won the Grand Prix at the Design Biennale in the Czech Republic. Often walking a tightrope between art and design, Victore uses his image-making as a means of getting ideas across by way of the brain, heart, or any other available organ. Using this methodology, Victore's work has recently expanded from book jackets, posters and promotional brochures to include Emmy award-winning animation for television.

below
Self promotional item for Victore Design Works. Designer, James Victore.

above
Halloween station identification for WVIT-TV, Hartford, CT. The 15-second holiday promotion "simply and eloquently cut through the quagmire of 'monster truck' television spots. In contrast to 98 percent of television spots, this was quiet, black and white, and very funny." The design won an Emmy Award. Designer, James Victore; art director, Brian Hall.

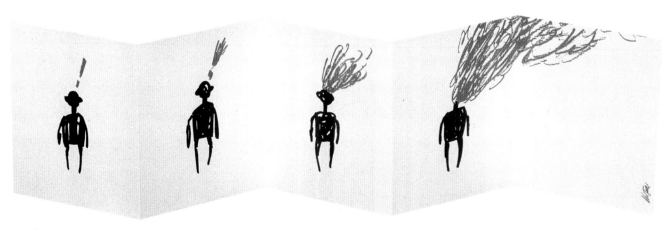

left
James Victore in his old
studio on 46th Street.
Photography,
Ray Charles White.

left
Self promotional postcard
for Victore Design Works.
Designer, James Victore.

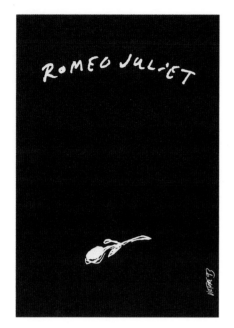

The Shakespeare Project *presents* Twelfth Night *or What You Will*, by Wm. Shakespeare. Admission is Free *Directed by* Scott Cargle. Our performances are; Central Park, Saturday June 11 at 12:00 PM and 4 PM. Sunday June 12 at 3:00 PM. Bryant Park, Sunday, June 19 and 26 at 3:00 PM. Fort Green Park, Brooklyn, Saturday, June 18 at 12:00 PM and 4:00 PM., and at The Henry Street Settlement, Abrons Art Center, Thursday, June 16 at 6:00 PM. Donations are greatly appreciated.

top
Romeo Juliet poster for The Shakespeare Project, New York, NY. An ongoing series of posters for free outdoor productions of Shakespeare's plays. The posters are made to entice, confuse, entertain and "...get butts in the seats," says Victore.
Designer, James Victore; art director, Scott Cargle.

bottom
Richard III poster for The Shakespeare Project. Designer, James Victore.

above
Twelfth Night poster for The Shakespeare Project. Designer, James Victore.

left
"Racism," a poster created to arouse discussion in the streets about racism. It won the Grand Prix at the 1994 Design Biennale in the Czech Republic.
Designer, James Victore.

far left and left
"Double Justice," a two-sided poster on racism and the death penalty for the National Association for the Advancement of Colored People and the American Civil Liberties Union, New York, NY. The poster served as a promotional piece for a documentary film and as an educational tool on its own. The design won a gold medal from the the New York Art Directors Club, and a silver medal at the 1994 Mexico Poster Biennale.
Designer, James Victore; writer, Kica Matos.

right
"Traditional Family Values" political poster for Post No Bills, New York, NY. The objective was to translate the 1992 Republican campaign rhetoric.
Designer, James Victore; art directors, Steven Brower, John Gall, Leah Lococo, Morris Taub and Susan Walsh.

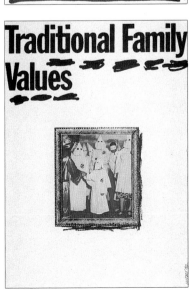

left
"Celebrate Columbus, 1492-1992," a poster created to counterbalance views during the 200th anniversary of Columbus' "discovery." It won a silver medal from the New York Art Directors Club, as well as the ICOGRADA Excellence prize at the Festival D'Affiches in Chaumont, France.
Designer, James Victore.

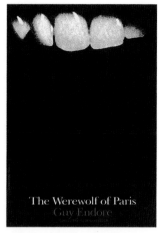

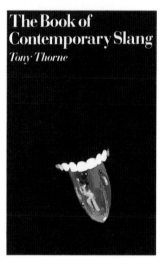

above
Book jacket design of *Johnny Got His Gun*, for Citadel Press. The design of the classic, anti-war tale was made to express the content of the book without being literal or decorative. Designer, James Victore.

top left
Book jacket design of *The Secrets of Love Magik*, for Citadel Press, New York, NY. This simple, absorbing cover separates the book from others on mysticism and witches without using the traditional "celestial" design.
Designer, James Victore.

middle left
Book jacket design of *Three Steps on the Ladder of Writing*, for Columbia University Press, New York, NY. The design of Cixous' name was meant to connote her fun, circus-like style of writing.
Designer, James Victore.

bottom left
Book jacket design of *The Crazy Green of Second Avenue*, for Citadel Underground, New York, NY. The imagery alludes to the funny and "very dirty" story.
Designer, James Victore.

top right
Book Jacket design of *The Werewolf of Paris*, for Citadel Underground.
Designer, James Victore.

middle right
Book jacket design of *Metapatterns*, for Columbia University Press. "The cover is an eloquent use of the very dry material included in the book," says Victore.
Designer, James Victore.

bottom right
Book jacket design of *The Book of Contemporary Slang*, for Times Books, New York, NY. "A colorful tongue... The humor was not appreciated. The design was killed," says Victore.
Designer, James Victore.

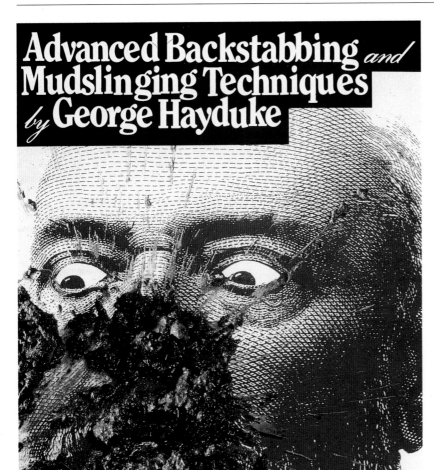

Advanced Backstabbing *and* Mudslinging Techniques *by* George Hayduke

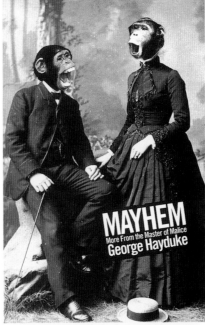

Book cover design of
Mayhem, for Lyle Stuart.
The second of the series.
Designer, James Victore.

left
Book cover design of
*Revenge Tactics From the
Master*, for Lyle Stuart.
The third of the series.
Designer, James Victore.

above
Book cover design of
*Advance Backstabbing and
Mudslinging Techniques*, for
Lyle Stuart, New York, NY.
The first of a series of designs
of Hayduke's books.
Designer, James Victore.

Vignelli Associates

Principals:
Massimo Vignelli,
Lella Vignelli, Yoshimi
Kono, David Law, Rebecca
Rose, Sharon Singer.
Year Founded: 1971
Size of Firm: 17
Key Clients: ABP/World
Trade Center, Amsterdam;
American Center in Paris;
Banca Promex, Mexico;
Bayerische Rück, Germany;
Benetton, worldwide;
Brooklyn Academy of
Music; COSMIT, Milan,
Italy; Solomon R.
Guggenheim Museum;
Kaltex Home, Mexico;
Rizzoli International
Publications; SEACO,
London; Zimmer and
Rohde, Germany.

475 Tenth Avenue
New York, NY 10018
212 244 1919

ignelli Associates has made significicant contributions to virtually every segment of the design field and has received international recognition through prizes, exhibitions and publications. Several of its designs are in the permanent collections of major museums. Originally based in Italy, Massimo and Lella Vignelli moved the center of their activities to New York in the mid-60's, and founded Vignelli Associates in 1971. The firm has set the standard for professional and versatile design, offering to an international clientele a complete range of design services, including graphic and corporate identity programs, publication design, packaging, environmental graphics, exhibitions and interiors, furniture and consumer products. One of the major concerns in the last few years has been the transformation of ordinary materials through design; limited resources push the creative effort to produce results that are both strong and appropriate to the task at hand. Scale, sequence and impact—always a mainstay of Vignelli graphic design—become ever-more important in creating design that is sensitive, highly communicative and timeless.

above
Communications program for COSMIT, Milan, Italy. The program, issued in four languages, includes complete corporate identity, promotional materials, brochures, folders, banners and signs. It was created to publicize and support a series of trade fairs in the areas of furniture, home furnishing, accessories and lighting. The central part of the program consists of fold-out brochures that provide a strong visual image for each of the trade fairs. The title and dates of the event are boldly printed on the outside, information is provided in the first fold, and the brochure, when fully opened, becomes a poster. Designers, Massimo Vignelli and Dani Piderman.

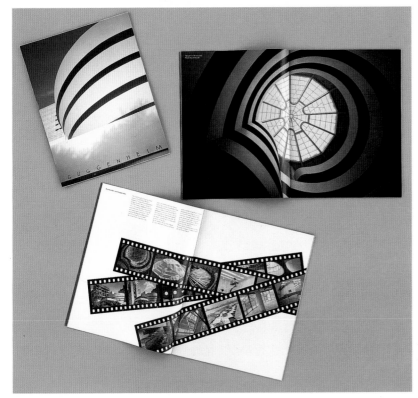

left
Guggenheim Museum Magazine, a quarterly publication of the museum. The magazine, mailed to museum members and distributed to bookstores nationwide, informs the public about the museum's activities, and always includes a central feature on the major current show. Playing with scale and sequence, the design results in impactful layouts and a strong image. Designers, Massimo Vignelli and Dani Piderman.

above
Graphics program for the Solomon R. Guggenheim Museum, New York, NY. The concept was to create a cohesive program that communicated the strength and energy of this cultural institution. Shown in the photo are the quarterly magazine, exhibition catalogs, annual report, museum guide, stationery, brochures and invitations. Designers, Massimo Vignelli and Dani Piderman.

right
Corporate identity and packaging program for Galerias Preciados department stores in Spain. In an effort to keep costs contained, the entire program was printed in one color. Impact and identity were given by the use of the simple "G" turned on its axis as the logo.
Designers, Massimo Vignelli and Lella Vignelli; client, Terron Schaefer.

right
Labels and cartons for wines produced by the Italian winery, Marchesi Fassati di Balzola. The labels were designed to blend with the color of the bottle and its contents. The unusual vertical layout of the label accommodates the length of the winery name while keeping the type large; it also makes the label easily readable when the wine is being poured. Cartons have bottles printed on the sides for mass display at the point of sale.
Designers, Massimo Vignelli and Dani Piderman.

below
Graphics program for American Center in Paris, France. The foldout brochures produce a large poster when fully opened, and each fold presents a different part of the message. The program is printed in two colors on inexpensive day-glow papers, giving the impression of multiple color printing while working within a contained budget. Designers, Massimo Vignelli and Rebecca Rose.

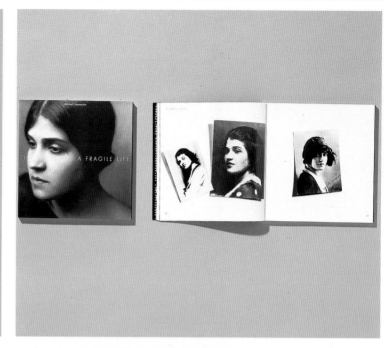

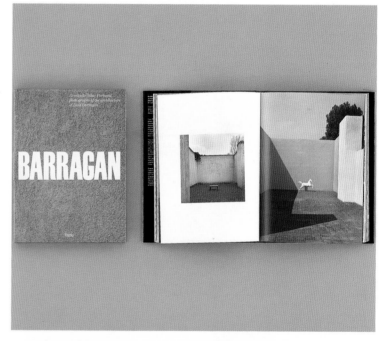

top left
Inside the Art World features a series of interviews with artists and art-world personalities, conducted by Barbaralee Diamondstein and published by Rizzoli. Snapshots taken during the interviews are placed in a band above each column of text to illustrate the dynamics of the conversation. Designers, Massimo Vignelli and Dani Piderman.

top right
Tina Modotti, book and jacket design for a new edition published by Chronicle Books, San Francisco. The book is an illustrated biography of one of the early 20th-century's most sensitive and powerful photographers. Designer, Massimo Vignelli.

middle left
Book and jacket design for a monograph on the New York-based architectural firm of Kohn Pederson Fox, published by Rizzoli, New York, NY. As with many architectural partnerships, KPF is known by its acronym, which Vignelli used as the main visual element on the cover to provide a strong identity.
Designers, Massimo Vignelli, with Abigail Strugis and Warren James coordinating for the publisher and architectural firm.

middle right
Book and jacket design for a monograph about the work of the great Mexican architect, Luis Barragan, published by Rizzoli. The cover of the book presents one of the signature Barragan walls. The brightly colored, rough-textured pink stucco creates the perfect background for the title of the book.
Designer and co-author, Massimo Vignelli.

bottom left
Book cover and design of *Anyone and Anywhere*, for Rizzoli. The books present the papers and round-table discussions generated at two conferences organized by ANY (Architecture New York). The books were printed in two colors, (red and black), on bright pink paper, and laid out with a lively sequence and varying scale of both type and images to create identity, interest and visual impact.
Designers, Massimo Vignelli; coordinator for ANY, Judy Gleib.

bottom right
Catalog design for *Fellini. I costumi e le mode* (*Fellini. Costumes and Fashion*), published by Charta, Milan, Italy. The catalog was the companion piece to an exhibition, also designed by Massimo, on costumes and fashions from Fellini's films. The book features large photographs, often double spreads, of scenes from the films; black pages with large white type mark the beginning of each chapter.
Designers, Massimo Vignelli and Michele Nason.

above
Catalog for the Eisenman/ Gehry exhibition at the Venice Biennale, 1991. The two architects represented the United States at the Fifth International Exhibition of Architecture of the Biennale, thus the choice of superimposing the two names to the American flag. The tabloid format used for an exhibition catalog allowed for the use of large plans and photographs of the projects and the architects at work.
Designers, Massimo Vignelli with Judy Gleib.

Waters Design

H_2O_s

Principals: John Waters,
Richard Whelan,
Margaret O'Donnell,
Michael Giangrasso,
Louis Medeiros
Year Founded: 1977
Size of Firm: 30
Key Clients:
Arrow Electronics,
Applied Microbiology,
Bacardi Limited,
Coopers & Lybrand,
Dow Jones, EDS, IBM,

Lucent Technologies,
MobileComm,
Renaissance Reinsurance,
Second Harvest,
The Wall Street Journal.

3 West 18th Street
New York, NY 10011
212 807 0717
www.watersdesign.com

aters Design develops corporate and brand identities, integrated marketing strategies and environmental design programs for small entrepreneurial customers and multi-market, international corporations. Since the early 1980s, Waters has been a leader in the use of electronic technologies for design and communications efficiency. Regardless of the medium, creating memorable messages is the goal of the firm. "We are not committed to style or technology, we're committed to ideas," Waters says. "Ideas that work. Ideas that create a spark in someone else's brain. Ideas that provoke a response." With recognitions and awards throughout the United States, Europe and Japan, Waters Design delivers finished products such as annual reports, employee magazines, CD-ROMs and interactive kiosks: but the "real product" is the generation of ideas and the management of information and activities required to bring these things to life.

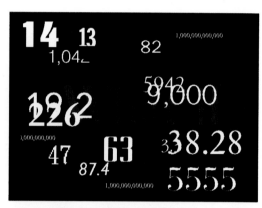

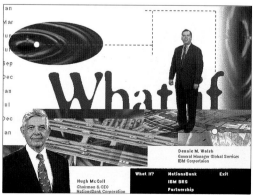

left
Interactive laptop presentation and companion printed brochure for L.P. Thebault, Parsippany, NJ. This CD-ROM focuses on time critical digital printing. A second CD highlights Thebault's traditional printing services and includes a plant tour. Design Manager, John Waters; designers, Colleen Syron, Dominic Poon and Jeanine Guido; illustrator/animator, Henry Kuo.

left
Still frames from *What If*, an interactive CD-ROM designed and produced for IBM Business Recovery Services, New York, NY. Used by both IBM and NationsBank (a partner in the project), the program conveys the importance of disaster recovery planning as well as IBM's partnership in risk management. Design Manager, John Waters; designer, Colleen Syron; programmer, Dominic Poon; animator, Henry Kuo; illustrator, Matt Beebe.

above
Logotype for the world's largest distributor of electronic components, Arrow Electronics, Melville, NY. Although designed in 1980, the worldwide identity standards were implemented in 1992. The cover of the 1994 annual report depicts the world's and Arrow's three dominant electronic markets. Design Manager, John Waters; designers, Waters, Linda Grimm and Elan Cole.

left
Logotype and interactive
multimedia show for Z-Cash,
and electronic product of
EDS Electronic Commerce,
Morris Plains, NJ. Still
frames from *Destination:
Convenience* introduced and
explained Z-Cash and other
products and services of
EDS to the banking industry.
Design Manager, Rick
Whelan; designers, Yeon
Hong and Dominic Poon;
programmers, Poon and
Henry Kuo.

above
Cover for *Lucent Magazine*,
a monthly publication for
the people of Lucent
Technologies, Inc., Murray
Hill, NJ.
Design Manager,
John Waters; designer,
John Paolini.

left
Coffee table book for
Bacardi Limited, Hamilton,
Bermuda. The book cele-
brates the union of two of
the world's oldest wine and
spirits companies, Bacardi
and Martini & Rossi.
Design Manager,
John Waters; designer,
Carol Bouyoucos.

Applied Microbiology, Inc.

1995 Annual Report

AMBI

left
Website architecture and
design for The Wall Street
Journal advertising sales
group, New York, NY. The
site is information rich, but
presented with a light touch.
Three characters, Joe
Journal, Media Mary and
Clyde Client, were created
to lead viewers to three
major areas of information.
Design Manager, John
Waters; designer, Colleen
Syron, illustrator, Vyto
Abraitis; programmer,
Dominic Poon.

above
1995 annual report for
Applied Microbiology, Inc.,
Tarrytown, NY. The cover
image continues a graphic
theme established in its
1994 report, mimicking a
corporate transformation
"as stunning as the meta-
morphosis of a caterpillar
into a butterfly."
Design Manager, Rich
Whelan; designer, Jeanine
Guido; illustrator, Bob Bleck.

Website architecture and design for Second Harvest, Chicago, IL. The site is designed as an interactive information center explaining the issue of hunger, attracting donations, supporting member food banks, reaching community agencies and recruiting others in the fight against hunger. Design Manager, Rick Whelan; designer, Michelle Novak; programmers, Dominic Poon, Armando Jimarez and Levana Cheng; photography, Tom Lindfors; illustrator, Mary Flockempa.

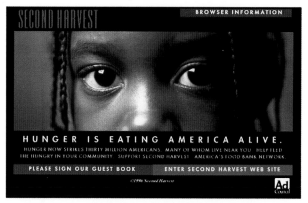

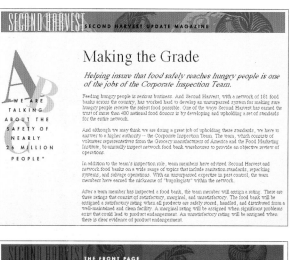

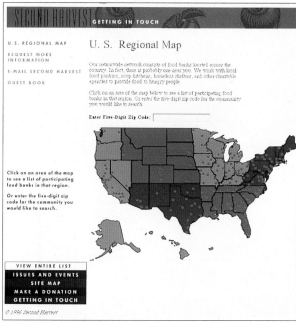

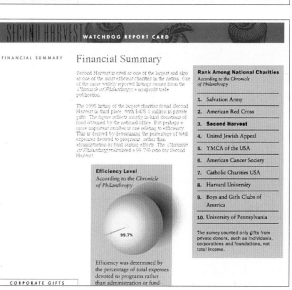

Three spreads from a
capabilities brochure
designed for Merrill Lynch
Custom Planning Services,
Princeton, NJ.
Design Manager, John
Waters; designer, Michelle
Novak; photography,
John Hill.

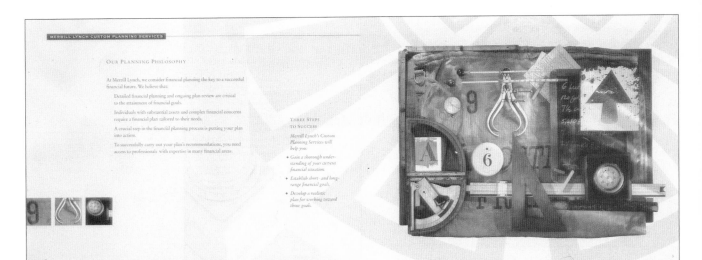

Wood Design

Principal: Tom Wood
Year Founded: 1990
Size of Firm: 4
Key Clients:
American Express,
Citibank,
Craig Cutler Studio,
Duke/Louis Dreyfus,
ITT Hartford,
Louis Dreyfus Group,
Raymond Mason,
New York Life,
Poetry Society of America,
RH Donnelly,
Max Roach,
Standard Rate and Data,
Richard Saul Wurman.

135 West 16th Street
Sixth Floor
New York, NY 10011
212 989 5295

Wood Design orchestrates ideas. A collaboration of ideas becomes a singular vision—teamwork without creative compromise. Curiosity, passion and undefined magic guide the process. Listening, feeling, seeing— a simplicity and clarity emerge to evoke response, motivation or cause. Discipline, detail and a committment to excellence in all areas of design.

The studio designs and consults for a wide range of clients, large and small, specializing in corporate identity, information design, literature programs, advertising and multimedia.

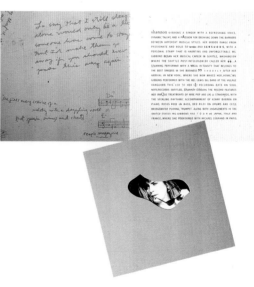

far right
Invitation booklet for jazz singer Shannon Gibbon mixes lyrical typography, collage and wine-stained pages in a nightclub spirit. Designers, Tom Wood and Alyssa Weinstein

right
Events calendar series for Poetry Society of America, New York, NY; designed in booklet format for easy implementation and economical production. Designers, Tom Wood and Alyssa Weinstein.

Brochure for Louis Dreyfus Energy documents world-wide assets and capabilities through a photographic essay, restrained typography, innovative diagrams, and contrasting paper stocks and materials.
Designers, Tom Wood and Alyssa Weinstein; photography, Jeff Corwin; illustrator, Wood.

A commemorative brochure that recreates Raymond Mason's sketchbook for his sculpture, The Departure of Fruits and Vegetables, and presents its evolution from pencil sketches and detailed watercolors to the finished piece. Designers, Tom Wood, Alyssa Weinstein and Clint Bottoni.

 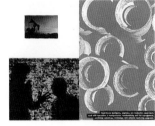 

right
Trade brochure for Louis Dreyfus Energy. The brochure utilizes typography and graphic images in provocative compositions to communicate industry contracts and technical information. Designers, Tom Wood and Alyssa Weinstein; photography, Jeff Corwin.

bottom
Louis Dreyfus Energy capabilities brochure and trade show booklet. Designers, Tom Wood and Alyssa Weinstein.

right
Annual report for Louis Dreyfus Natural Gas reinforces the concept of consistent growth using a question and answer format, topographic maps and illustrated facts. Designers, Tom Wood and Alyssa Weinstein; photography, Gloria Baker; illustrator, Clint Bottoni.

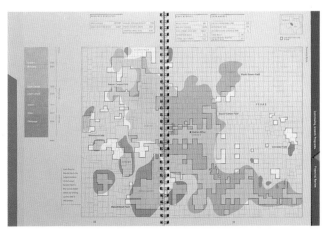 

Promotional booklet for
Craig Cutler Studio. By
contrasting color and black
and white images from all
over the world, juxtaposing
subject matter, scale and
multilanguage text, Cutler's
versatility as an accomplished
studio and location photographer is achieved.
Designers, Tom Wood,
Alyssa Weinstein and
Mayda Freije; photography,
Craig Cutler.

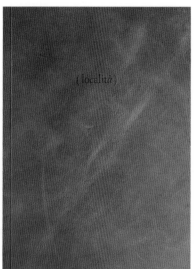

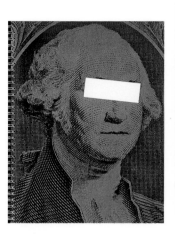

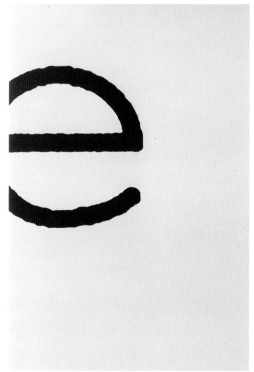

top
AIGA/NY seminar workbook
"Money and Contracts";
Promotional booklet for
Craig Cutler Studio.
Designers, Tom Wood and
Alyssa Weinstein.

bottom
Louis Dreyfus Energy
capabilities brochure and
trade show booklet.
Designers Tom Wood,
Alyssa Weinstein.